Gift *of* Soul,
Gift *of* Wisdom

Gift *of* Soul, Gift *of* Wisdom

A Spiritual Resource
for Mentoring and Leadership

RABBI BRADLEY SHAVIT ARTSON

Published by Behrman House, Inc.
Springfield, NJ 07081
www.berhmanhouse.com

Designed by Howard Levy / Red Rooster Group, NY
Manufactured in the United States of America

Library of Congress Cataloging-In-Publication Data

Artson, Bradley Shavit
The Gift of Soul, Gift of Wisdom: A Spiritual Resource for Mentoring & Leadership /
Bradley Shavit Artson
p. cm
ISBN 0-87441-643-4
1. Mentoring–Religious aspects–Judaism. 2. Leadership–Religious aspects–Judaism.
I. Title.

BM729.M45A78 2006
296.6'1—dc22

2005037142

To my children, Jacob and Shira

הן נאין ומעשיהם נאים ולבן לשמים
סופרים יה:ה

To my wife, Elana

חברתי ואשת בריתי
מלאכי וכתובה עתיקה

To my father, David

כנפשך. זה אביך
ספרי דברים, פרשת ראה

ALSO BY BRADLEY SHAVIT ARTSON

Love Peace and Pursue Peace:
A Jewish Response to War and Nuclear Annihilation

It's a Mitzvah! Step-by-Step to Jewish Living

Making a Difference: Putting Jewish Spirituality into Action,
One Mitzvah at a Time

The Bedside Torah: Wisdom, Visions, and Dreams

Dear Rabbi: Jewish Answers to Life's Questions

Contents

Preface

This is a book about leadership and mentoring and why we must have both in order to sustain and nurture the Jewish community. Its lessons draw on the rich resources of Judaism's sacred texts and spiritual heritage for inspiration. I first considered writing this book during a time when I was conversing with educators, lay leaders, teachers, volunteers, therapists, and rabbis about what is necessary for Jewish continuity and community. Jewish communal life today is blessed with a marvelous array of informative books, Jewish institutions, and learned scholars. What is missing more than anything else is affective and spiritual leadership: we train our leaders and mentors to convey information but not necessarily to cultivate open souls. We hone the intellect yet neglect to nurture the spirit. And intelligence is never enough. As Elisabeth Kübler-Ross understood, "Knowledge helps, but knowledge alone is not going to help anybody. If you do not use your head and your heart and your soul, you are not going to help a single human being."[1]

To give the gift of soul, *b'hachmah bitvunah uv'da'at*,[2] means to cultivate and to serve God's creatures through wisdom and understanding. As guides (leaders and mentors), we assist by embodying the values and practices that Judaism holds dear and by sharing our journey through life with other people, our *talmidim*, our disciples.

Only by opening ourselves—flawed and striving—to another person's gaze do we express Judaism's conviction that people can change (and improve) and that imperfect people are worthy of love (ours and God's).

It should be noted here that there is no single term in English to describe this model of sharing wisdom, skills, and experience to encourage others to become the best possible version of themselves. The best I can do is use the word *mentor* to cover the range of roles undertaken by one who midwifes cognitive, emotional, and spiritual growth: one who guides, teaches, leads, advises, counsels, instructs, supervises, and coaches. In Jewish tradition, such an integrated model is one's *rebbe*.

More than mere conduits of information and skills, mentors may offer their love, trust, and affirmation to those willing to accept them. They use their warmth and affection as tools for inspiring passionate Jewish living and leadership. To mentor is to share a passion for Judaism and Jewish communal institutions. To mentor is to open our lives to other people, reach out with affection, and offer ourselves as inspiration, confidant, and guide. Far from relying on title or institutional affiliation, a mentor uses gifts of soul and heart to encourage other seeking souls, to provide a spiritual context to the knowledge and wisdom offered by the Torah and its traditions. In addition to strengthening communities and institutions, a mentor engages one person at a time. The mentor refuses to divorce leadership from caring, informing from inspiring. Above all, the mentor addresses another's whole self by offering his or her whole self in the relationship. As we are taught in Jewish tradition:

> A person's rebbe is defined as one who teaches wisdom and not one who has taught the written and oral Torah. This is Rabbi Meir's opinion. Rabbi Yehudah taught, "Whoever has taught most of the student's wisdom." Rabbi Yosei says, "Even if the rebbe did no more than make the student's eyes light up from an explanation of a single selection from the oral Torah, that teacher is still considered to be the student's rebbe."[3]

Anyone in a position to teach, counsel, and advise others is already a mentor. And anyone willing to invest the effort can become a better mentor. All it takes is openness, readiness, and a love of other people. Rabbis, cantors, educators, youth leaders, teachers, counselors, lay leaders, and volunteers—all can fill this vital role. Indeed, the greater our formal education, the greater the effort it may take to learn to mentor, since we have been so blinded and distorted by our infatuation with Western modes of learning. In high schools and universities, we are systematically rewarded for the kind of knowledge that can be reproduced for a test or reduced to a footnote. Jewish learning aspires to a loftier, less tangible goal: crafting a mensch (a good, well-balanced, caring person) in the service of the sacred.

My hope is that this book will encourage potential mentors. It will challenge us to return to authentic Jewish modes of leading and mentoring. These traditional methods unite the cognitive, affective, and spiritual and address the heart, mind, and soul as if they were one. If we hope to live balanced lives, we can do no less. As the Western world embraces the insights of a gentler holistic teaching (embodied in such diverse and rich fields as object-relations and social-constructionist psychology, postmodernist philosophy and literary criticism, social history, women's and gender studies), the insights of classical Jewish teaching finally may enjoy a broader hearing, anticipating, as they do, so many of the insights of this emerging consensus. This book will offer a way to reclaim those teachings and liberate character formation and community building from the constricting bonds of outmoded academic values.

The introduction sets the stage, offering a panoramic view of the way modernity has substituted systems for people, created departments in place of more holistic learning. Building on that broad contextualization, the first two chapters of the book focus on our contemporary need for mentors, as well as their historical context. Why do we need them, and how are they rooted in the classical sources? Chapter 1, "The Contemporary Challenge: Finding Our Way Back Home from the Wilderness of Modernity," examines the unhealthy way in which our culture often separates knowledge and wisdom into distinct realms, to the detriment of student and mentor alike. It discusses how we can heal that rift by returning to the ancient Jewish model of mentor and *talmid*. Chapter 2, "The Jewish Way to Transmit Wholeness and Wisdom," presents a Jewish model for guidance that is simultaneously nurturing, involving, and informing. It highlights some classical mentors, focusing first on the ultimate leader, Moses, and then on some of the great teachers of the Talmud. Some readers may find their embracing style of mentoring antiquated, but I hope to show that their kind of mentorship is both relevant and well within our grasp.

Part II, "Leaders and Mentors in Today's World," moves from theory to application, considering who Jewish mentors are today, what it is that mentors do, and what makes a good mentor effective. Chapter 3, "Parents: The Quintessential Mentors," illustrates the deep analogies between being a mentor and being a parent. In Chapter 4, "Other Mentors," we broaden our search for nurturing guides to learn from spouses, teachers, employers, colleagues, and the community at large. The range of potential mentors is endless.

Part III, "Becoming Better Leaders and Mentors," launches the practical part of the book. Here we explore ways in which each of us can become a more helpful and effective mentor. Of course the fundamental question, "Can anyone be a mentor?" (the answer is yes!), deserves explicit consideration, which it gets in Chapter 5, "Can Anyone Be a Mentor?" Those readers interested in a more philosophical approach may well enjoy this chapter. In Chapter 6, "The Virtues of a Mentor," we consider the character traits needed for an effective counselor: temperament, pedagogy, and soul. In Chapter 7, we focus on "A Mentor's Communication Skills." Those skills coalesce around two broad areas: communing and communicating. Communing involves the emotional shelter a mentor must provide in order for the protégé to feel safe enough to risk openness and growth. The first topic of the chapter is how to enhance this sense of caring. But the emotional context is only the beginning, and a mentor must translate a nonverbal welcome into words; a mentor must communicate. Without the mentor's active listening, the mentored one cannot know that he or she has been heard and understood. This chapter suggests Jewish sources and practical guidelines to help mentors improve their listening skills. It also examines the moral guidelines Judaism offers for proper speech (*sh'mirat halashon*), and it looks at ways of enhancing trust through better communication.

Part IV, "Roadblocks on a Mentor's Path," explores the challenges and frustrations that arise in any intimate relationship. Chapter 8, "When a Mentor Is Wounded," opens the discussion of the challenges and disappointments that accompany spiritual mentoring. Chapter 9, "Conflicts Due to a Mentor's Role," offers suggestions for coping with the bruises and disappointments that a role of spiritual mentorship invites. Chapter 10, "When Expectations and Reality Clash," continues that exploration, examining the gap between ideal visions and their embodiment in an imperfect reality.

Part V concludes with Chapter 11, "Who Heals the Healers?," which suggests sources of strength and renewal for those willing to do the sacred work of guiding and nurturing seeking souls.

According to the medieval sages, the crown of all wisdom is theology, the search for an understanding of God. With that notion in mind, we offer an appendix, "With Abounding Love: A Theology for the Whole Heart," that articulates a theological understanding of relationship as a key metaphor for the connection linking God, Judaism, and community. This essay is offered as a resource for those seeking a philosophical base for their work as mentors, locating the topic of how to become a role model and guide on the broader Jewish agenda of our Covenant with God and Torah.

"Reading List for Mentors (and Mentors-to-Be)" recommends titles for further reading, and the glossary provides definitions of the important Hebrew and Judaic terms used in the text. All terms in the glossary are also defined at their first appearance in the text.

Perhaps an explanation is appropriate here. This book reflects the thoughts and perceptions of a rabbi who has worked in both a congregation and a university. Although I have attempted to include perspectives and examples representing different aspects of communal life—those of Federation and agency executives, lay leaders and volunteers, cantors, educators, and committee members—I can't help but see the world through my own eyes. That means that many of the perspectives and examples come from my experience and from the experiences of other rabbis. All of the anecdotes reported are true, but the names, characteristics, and identities of the participants have been altered to preserve their privacy. I hope that the insights illumined by the mentors in these stories are relevant and helpful to others in leadership and mentoring roles. Similarly, although this book is written from the perspective of Torah and Judaism, I believe its lessons apply to all people who seek to build communities in which the spirit can thrive.

A technical note: Israel is biblical shorthand for the Hebrew *am Yisrael* עם ישראל (the people Israel), meaning the Jewish people. I use the term to convey that sense.

• • •

As with the writing of any book, there are many people to thank. I am deeply grateful to Behrman House for its steady and generous support and encouragement. David Behrman proved as persistent and skilled (and patient and demanding) an editor as he is a devoted and supportive friend. His guidance, support, and suggestions were instrumental as I began this project. I look forward to a lifelong friendship and association with him and with the house that bears his family's name.

It is, also, a special pleasure to thank Sunny Yudkoff, who stepped in as editor, advisor, and colleague and turned a rough manuscript into a polished book. She possesses deep vision, patient skill, and a knowing heart. It has been a joy to work with her and learn from her.

This book owes much to the good people who gave it their careful attention. I am particularly grateful to those who read drafts of the work in progress. The meticulous editing of Dr. Joan Kaye, executive director of the Bureau of Jewish Education in Orange County, California, greatly strengthened the book. I am also grateful to my dear friend and gifted colleague Rabbi Elie Kaplan Spitz, whose close reading was but one of innumerable acts of brotherly love. My deepest thanks to two past presidents of Congregation Eilat, my caring mentors Debbie Sirkin and David Kennedy, who valiantly shielded their rabbi, making it possible for me to conduct research and write. Above all, I owe thanks to those members of Congregation Eilat who read and edited each chapter and were willing to critique their rabbi's writing and thinking: Cheryl Altman, Howard Altman, Rabbi Mark Ankcorn, Patricia Baker, Ann Bialy, Judy Buckser, Fannie Emmer, Julie Fine, Ingrid Gallin, Valerie Hamilton, Rosalyn Hirsch, Lauren Kelner, Dr. Deborah Kirschbaum, David Lorch, Jennifer Most, Jack Pariser, Leah Pariser, Richard Penkava, Floris Pittler, Sarah Robinson, Muriel Rosenkranz, Brenda Vann, Brian Wright, and Fay Zeramby.

While the final drafts of this book were maturing, I came to serve as the dean of the Ziegler School of Rabbinic Studies and vice president of the University of Judaism in Bel-Air, California. I am reminded daily of the blessing of working with an outstanding group of people: students, faculty, administration, and lay leaders. My deepest thanks go to the university's president, Rabbi Robert Wexler, who is both mentor and friend, and to my beloved students—rabbis and soon-to-be rabbis. It is a privilege and a joy to work at such a *makom Torah* מקום תורה (place of Torah learning).

My continuing thanks and affection also go to the Jewish Theological Seminary, where I was ordained as a rabbi and where I still cherish my friendships and many close ties to faculty, administration, and students.

I owe deep thanks also to the Wexner Heritage Foundation. Through it, I was given the chance to explore the ideas in this book with remarkable people in idyllic settings. American Jewry is better because of the Jewish education and deeper connection to Judaism provided by the Wexner Foundation to select Jews all across North America. I especially want to thank Larry Moses, Rabbi Nathan Laufer, Rabbi Shoshana Gelfand, and Rabbi Jay Moses for their insights and help over the years.

The clinical staff of the Jewish Family Services of Orange County, California, joined in a monthly seminar on counseling and Jewish values, carefully critiquing an early draft of this book. The finished product is richer because of the careful reading and wisdom of Mel Roth, executive director, Judy Glickman Zevin, clinical supervisor, and Bara Samon, Heather Watson, and Adrienne Cohen, staff counselors. I am grateful to each of them.

My deepest thanks to Maria Lara for all the care and assistance she extended to me and my family—especially my children.

It is a joy to be able to thank Hank and Lillian Rubin, who were mentors during my teen and college years and are now dear friends.

Of course my beloved family has provided a constant backdrop of love and support. I am deeply grateful to my mother, Barbara Friedman Artson; my sister and sister-in-law, Tracy and Dawn Osterweil-Artson; my niece, Sydney, and my nephew, Benjamin; my brother, Matthew Artson; my father-in-law, Reuben Shavit; and Grace Mayeda, my beloved nanny.

My father, David Artson, and I have journeyed far together. Warm childhood memories of laughter, spontaneity, and generosity of soul sustained me even through times when our relationship was strained. Thank God we are able now to revel in our affection and our closeness. My father is an unfailing source of love and encouragement for me, Elana, and our children. His humor and his easy presence are blessings for which I will be always grateful.

My children, Jacob and Shira, fill me with profound joy and purpose. They teach me so much about laughing, loving, and sharing. They embody the best values of Torah, and their love for each other, their family, and their friends provides a model that I aspire to match. Their gifts of soul make them little rebbes already. I pray that they will grow to embrace that role with gratitude and gusto.

My beloved wife, Elana, is my rebbe in every sense: her willingness to open her soul and share her abundant supply of wisdom, warmth, honesty, and love has led me to places I could never have imagined possible. Her embodiment of the Jewish values of *ahavah, tz'ni'ut, and rahamim* (love, modesty, and compassion) mark her as a treasure as a wife and as a worthy daughter of Abraham and Sarah. She is my best friend.

To Elana, Shira, Jacob, and my father, I lovingly dedicate this book.

Aharon aharon haviv—I am grateful beyond words to the Holy One, the Mentor of mentors, listening ear, affirming heart, source of all wisdom: you have shared of your wisdom and caring with your creatures so that we might participate in your work of nurturing one another. I pray that this book will in some small way refract your divine love and allow it to shine on others more brightly.

תם ונשלם שבה לאל בורא עולם
Tam Ve-Nishlam Shevah le-El Borei Olam

Bradley Shavit Artson
Los Angeles, California

Leaders & Mentors in Our History, in Our Tradition, in Our Lives

An Invitation

Almost all of us who care about Judaism and our community can recall an older relative or neighbor who fashioned our precious memories of Jewish holy days, Sabbaths, and festivals. Whether we were born Jewish or have chosen to be Jewish, we all have been touched by that special someone who invited us to a Seder, shared an afternoon to bake hallah, or persuaded us to attend a community event. Our Judaism is not merely learned. It is lived.

The foundation of Jewish belonging is built one brick at a time, person to person. However effective our classes on Judaism, however inclusive our institutions, the key component of transmitting a love of yiddishkeit and Torah is one Jew willing to share time and wisdom with another seeking soul. In the words of a medieval proverb, "What comes from the heart enters the heart."

The personal attention of a mentor to a willing student has perpetuated Torah and Jewish identity in every age. That power of the individualized transmission makes good psychological sense: we are drawn to communities in which we feel welcomed and valued, particularly if those communities offer profundity, beauty, and goodness. This connection between mentor and protégé is the glue that binds communities, but it does far more than that. Individual connection makes theological sense, too. The Torah portion "Hayei Sarah" begins with the statement that "Sarah's lifetime—the span of Sarah's life—came to 127 years. Sarah died in Kiryat Arba."[1] A few verses earlier in the Torah, we are offered the seemingly unconnected information that "Milkah too had borne children to your brother Nahor . . . (including Bethuel), Bethuel being the father of Rebecca."[2] Even though Rebecca and Sarah don't meet personally, the looming figure of Sarah remains a powerful and nurturing presence through her legacy and example. Sarah's legacy mentors Rebecca, and the story of the two matriarchs in turn mentors us, their sons and daughters, across the ages.

Why does the Torah tell us about the birth of Rebecca (Sarah's future daughter-in-law) prior to informing us of the death of Sarah? The sages of the Midrash explain this juxtaposition by referring to a curious line from the biblical book of Kohelet: "The sun also rises and the sun sets."[3]

> Rabbi Abba said, "Don't we know that the sun rises and the sun sets? But the meaning is that prior to causing the 'sun' of one righteous person to set, the Holy One causes the 'sun' of another *tzedek* to rise. . . . Before the Holy Blessing One[4] allowed Sarah's sun to set, God caused that of Rebecca to rise."[5]

Before allowing Sarah to die, God had already assured the steadying presence of another matriarch through the birth of Rebecca, indicating that the health of the Jewish community could not continue without the perpetuation of a loving embodiment of its warmth and wisdom. The example set by Sarah—her dedication to her family and her strong-willed personality—is translated and extended by Rebecca.

So it is in every generation. We are Jewish today because of the loving coaches we encountered along the way: grandparents, rabbis, parents, siblings, friends, neighbors, teachers, and acquaintances. Their willingness to reach out to us, to include us in their holy-day celebrations, to walk us through the labyrinth of communal leadership, to work with us on a worthy project, or to teach us the fundamentals of Torah and its values—those efforts are the reasons we know from the inside how wonderful it is to be a Jew. The people who made those efforts are our mentors.

Because someone cared enough to give us the experiences of Jewish living, our minds are now tuned in to the sacred cycles of the seasons and the Sabbaths. Because someone made the effort to allow us to assume a leadership role, we found a path for activism and belonging. Because someone touched our hearts through Jewish music or drama, the melodies of our Jewish lives resonate so deeply.

How can we ever repay those mentors? Our mentors may no longer be available to us, but we can still show them just how much we value what they taught us. We can pass their gift—the gift of soul—to those whose lives we touch. We can become a mentor to someone else.

Before the sunset fades, the new sun rises. Perhaps you know of someone who is interested in converting to Judaism. Maybe you know a Jew who has never experienced the warmth and beauty of a Shabbat service and a meal afterward. Perhaps your organization needs the skills that a younger colleague or neighbor possesses or you know of a younger person who could use an open ear. You can make the connection. Someone reached out to involve each one of us; now it's our turn to reach out to tomorrow's leaders.

Your warmth can light their path. You can be their role model and friend. You can be their mentor.

Chapter One

The Contemporary Challenge

Finding our Way Back Home
from the Wilderness of Modernity

> *It is true that scientific knowledge raises a person, pro-*
> *vides wings to soar to great heights, enlightens the eyes*
> *to discover the secrets of nature and to utilize its powers,*
> *to make life more pleasant and to increase longevity.*
> *General knowledge also endows a person with spiritual*
> *powers. But all the acquisitions of general knowledge are*
> *vessels that help one to live—and are not life itself. . . .*
> *The goal of life is . . . to know the God of the universe, to*
> *walk in God's ways, and to cling to God.*
> —Rabbi Benzion Uziel, Michmanei Uziel

There is nothing more precious than a human being. Each person embodies a portal to a better tomorrow. No computer is as complex as a human being, no novel as nuanced. This most extraordinary of creations requires a special kind of mentoring to flourish and to contribute to the world's repair. All people, both Jew and gentile, have this potential and share this need, whether or not the potential is realized and the need is fulfilled. Our most important wisdom—our sense of how to be decent, how to be moral, how to care—we learn through imitation. Life is an apprenticeship in the art of being human.

Rebbe is the Hebrew term for the holistic teacher who shapes and guides the whole person. While the term historically denotes a teacher of Torah,[1] the title has evolved within Jewish tradition to distinguish those special mentors whose goal is nothing less than to inspire a life well lived. While Jews cherish the Torah Scroll as the indispensable guide to living a full life, it is the Torah *as embodied in the deeds and teachings of a mentor* that makes the greatest impact on the molding of Jewish souls.[2] Accordingly, love for one's mentor flows into a love for God, Torah, and Israel. And love from one's mentor nourishes this stream. *The Gift of Soul* focuses on the mentoring described in Jewish sources and undertaken from a Jewish perspective. This book proposes that Jewish continuity depends not on glitzy programs and catchy slogans but on producing mentors in greater numbers. The future of Judaism requires us to do what we can.

While our discussion relies primarily on the Bible and other Jewish sources, we harvest insights that apply to people of all faiths. Many of those insights find parallel expression in humanity's other traditions and faiths. Anyone can offer direction, courage, and wisdom along the path of life. Although the following chapters primarily address Jews who would mentor other Jews, the insights offered here can assist all people to mentor others. You don't have to be Jewish to be this kind of mentor.

Often a mentor is a relative. Today, for example, Jon Stern is a successful chef. Once an officer of his congregation, he now serves on the board of a national synagogue organization. Ask him how he came to show calm in the face of pressure, how he came by his commitment to service and community, and he talks about one special influence: his grandfather. He remembers his grandfather sending him to a Jewish summer camp year after year. And he recalls his grandfather listening with pride as he practiced his Torah portion for his bar mitzvah celebration. Jon shared with me stories of the hours his grandfather spent with him when he was young and suggested that his admiration for his grandfather provided the drive he needed to be able to succeed in life. When it came to identifying the one responsible for giving wings to his soul, Jon didn't single out an institution. Jon is grateful to his grandfather, who taught him what it means to be a mensch and provided him with an enduring connection to Judaism.

Jon's openness to being mentored as a child is not unique. While we may owe a share of gratitude to schools, congregations, summer camps, and other institutions, our choices and actions in life are influenced by those caring people who demonstrate their faith in us, who give of their time, and who regale us with their life experiences. Those soul guides, those mentors, allow us to become who we are.

Nothing can substitute for such people. It is precisely their fusion of heart, mind, and soul that makes Jewish continuity and personal growth possible. In difficult times in the past, they have given us courage and confidence. In today's difficult times, we must transmit their rich bequest to the people who look to us for guidance, wisdom, and renewal.

The Best of Times, the Worst of Times

The last few centuries have produced unsurpassed levels of material wealth as well as outstanding scientific and medical advances. Our globe has become a community as people have achieved the ability to connect with and learn about one another. Human freedom to communicate, travel, and live where and how we choose continues to transform what used to be destiny into personal choice. Once it was possible to be the master of the broad sum of human knowledge. Aristotle was both philosopher and scientist; the Rambam (Rabbi Moses ben Maimon, or Maimonides), was physician, legal scholar, theologian, and communal leader. Today there is so much knowledge to master that our education often seems to teach us more and more about less and less. A lack of breadth makes it harder to see the big picture and harder to remember that the purpose of an education will always be more than professional training. Education ought to entail an exposure to the great ideas, virtues, and insights that ennoble human life. As the ancient rabbis said, "The adornment of knowledge is wisdom."[3]

Perhaps this modern focus on the compartmentalization of knowledge is compensation in part for the collapse of old certainties. The brittle truths that restrained our terror of the unknown (such as medieval religious doctrine or the nineteenth century's dogma of individualism, progress, and science) have crumbled before the abundance of our searching, questioning, and openness. Few of us would seek to return to the earlier ignorance or superstition, but the new knowledge comes at a cost. Knowing that the cosmos is fifteen billion years old can be both liberating and unnerving! Greater access to information offers us the possibility of greater understanding even as it underscores that this is a time of contrasts: some feast while others starve. Democracy thrives while terrorism remains a serious threat in every corner of the world. Technology gives us unprecedented capabilities—and access to pornography, bigotry, and violence. The staggering volume of information and knowledge—whose benefits we enjoy every day—makes it that much harder to distinguish between the significant and the trivial. All those choices offer us fresh options for tailoring our lives to fit the contours of our interests and talents. But the availability of choice can also make our values and priorities appear idiosyncratic and petty. Knowing that the world is so massive can make moral judgments seem quaint. As Richard Dawkins of Oxford University conceded, in a world governed by "blind physical forces and genetic replication, some people are going to get hurt, others are going to get lucky, and you won't find any rhyme or reason for it."[4]

Lacking the certainty of previous generations (and their saints) makes it even more vital to muster a sense of purpose. Some respond to the threat of rootlessness by seeking sanctuary in the fundamentalism of earlier times. Some seek the false security of idealizing an earlier age or cloistering their minds in the doctrine of literalist belief, whether religious or secular. But most people today will not retreat from the liberating benefits of this age of choice. Most of us seek ways in which to integrate new levels of freedom and pluralism into lives of meaning and depth. We don't want to retreat from modernity; we want to deepen modernity. Blights of poverty, ignorance, and injustice that continue to demand our attention are evidence of a deeper spiritual dislocation. We don't know what to *do* with our freedom. We have not yet been able to mobilize ourselves and our culture to live up to the potential of our age. The answer, of course, is not to jettison freedom, nor is it to retreat from our godlike ability to choose who we will become. Instead, we are called to harness to the service of our highest possibilities—lives of meaning and communities of compassion and justice—the human talent unleashed by freedom.

The Western Dichotomy Between Knowledge and Wisdom

As the task of understanding our place in the world becomes more complex, one powerful response is to shy away from uncertainty, to focus on what can be known. We can test for mastery of facts; we cannot grade the depth of another's compassion. So our examinations too often focus on the illusory comfort of what can be measured, weighed, or quantified. But in the process, we confuse knowledge with wisdom. Some contemporary thinkers, assuming we can know only what we can physically perceive, reduce the cosmos to empty space and swirling gas. That redefinition of reality as material reality brings us perilously close to reducing the issues of living to a technical fix. As Professor James Jones warns:

> After Newton, everywhere men went, they listened for (and therefore heard) nothing but the hum of machinery. Modernity's goal was to

transform the world into a technological problem. One by one the tasks of governing the state, healing the sick, guiding the economy, choosing right and wrong, and understanding human nature became "sciences"—that is, governed by measurement and the desire for control.[5]

One response to complex and irreducible mysteries is to retreat within the tangible and the material. We mistake expertise for profundity and then become disappointed when great skill doesn't always equal moral depth, compassion, or sensitivity. The very structure of Western education often betrays the division of learning into two categories: the acquisition of skills and facts, which we assign to our school systems and universities, and character formation and moral development, processes we pass off as a supplementary activities at best and relegate to youth groups, parents, or religious schools. The talents we most reward and revere are in the first category.

In fairness, most schools, seminaries, and universities do assume a mystical connection between knowledge, moral integrity, and spiritual depth. Somehow by studying a variety of subjects and mastering the skill of critical thinking, a student is expected to be able to make moral distinctions *and* develop the values that make for committed citizenship. While our education system succeeds at teaching most students how to think and how to write, it remains troubled regarding the transmission or cultivation of moral virtues. Few academic requirements explicitly address moral or developmental concerns. No one measures how or whether the ability to scan Romantic poetry or explain quantum mechanics encourages volunteering in a homeless shelter or heightens one's awe at the sight of the Grand Canyon. As the poet Alan Shapiro reminds us (and what he says about art is true of all knowledge):

> To enrich perception isn't necessarily to make perception more amenable to virtue, or to a particular moral code. Nor is it to make us any happier, for in heightening consciousness of what it means to be

alive, poetry and art in general can overwhelm us with how brief, uncertain, and unredeemably painful life so often is.[6]

Americans exhibit great ambivalence about teaching values in school. They debate whose values are to be taught and express concern over the school's assumption of a role once assigned to parents. Greater weight is placed on academic learning, which counts toward career and promotion in that career, than is placed on values, which do not. That emphasis undermines a more holistic scholastic approach even when one is offered. What are cultivated as goals in Western education, from kindergarten through graduate school, are competence and skepticism. Two decades of schooling successfully inculcates a focus on mastering facts and manipulating tools. That focus allows for a great gap in the areas that most require persistent education: moral development, gratitude, and compassion. We learn to compare and contrast, but we are not trained to harmonize and synthesize. We do not rehearse creativity, nor do we practice building connections. The physicist David Scott, former chancellor of the University of Massachusetts at Amherst, noted, "Modernism has directed exhaustive objective focus on the world as a database, but excluded anything having to do with meaning. This causes wisdom to drop out of favor as a goal of education."[7] We teach people to have a career, but we don't prepare them to live a life. Loneliness, cynicism, and materialism are the logical results of an understandable attempt to restore confidence in the world around us. The motivation may be reasonable, but the result is shallow and unworthy.

There is another way.

Instead of responding to complexity and uncertainty by blinding ourselves to an impoverished materialism, rather than simplifying existence by ignoring what cannot be mastered, we might admit that life is inevitably contradictory, complex, and confusing. There is more to reality than we yet know. In the face of ambiguity, closing our eyes and averting our gaze are not solutions. What we need is a living guide to give coherence to the possibilities, perceptions, and positions, someone who has walked a little farther down that road called life, someone who can point out the pitfalls and the shortcuts along the way.[8] In the words of Rabbi Samson Raphael Hirsch, the nineteenth century German leader of Neo-Orthodoxy, "Torah knowledge cannot be acquired from books alone. Masters are needed to teach it."[9] We crave someone who will teach us to walk with our eyes open, who will encourage us to celebrate the mystery and the marvel rather than collude in the misguided attempt to ignore or categorize it.

We need guides, partners willing to share their insights, their questions, their shortcomings, and their faith. We need mentors.

Chapter Two

The Jewish Way to Transmit Wholeness and Wisdom

> *Rav Kahana once went in and hid under Rav's (his rebbe's) bed. He heard him chatting and joking [with his wife] and doing what he required. . . . [Rav] said to him, "Kahana, are you here? Go out because it is rude." He replied, "This too is Torah, and I need to learn it."*
>
> —B'RACHOT

Instead of ignoring the layers of knowledge beyond the reach of the scientific method, instead of restricting ourselves to the experiences we can quantify, let us embrace an approach that will allow us to ask *all* our questions and celebrate a reality we can never master. By exploring the cosmos in an intuitive and spiritual way, we provide ourselves with far broader vistas for wisdom and depth.[1] By supplementing learning with our logic and our words, we can teach ourselves to understand through our entire being. The kabbalists refer to this expanded form of learning as *sucking*, what a calf does to ingest its mother's milk. This holistic approach is much more demanding, as it requires the gifts of presence and time. To nurture a whole person with a rich blend of emotional depth, spiritual wealth, and intellectual acumen demands a guide willing to offer himself or herself as a tool for learning and love. The mentor is such a guide, participating in an education as variegated and overflowing as life itself.

This age-old Jewish experiential approach to integrating wisdom has recently gained allies from other disciplines. In psychoanalysis, for example, the hierarchical therapist-client relationship is being drastically reconfigured. The Freudian model dictates that the therapist offers a blank slate onto which the patient can project internal fantasies. The role of the therapist is to then listen and offer authoritative analysis of the meaning of the patient's projections. Far from offering reciprocity, the therapist hides behind a professional veneer, and that distance is viewed as essential if any psychotherapy is to occur. Thankfully, many psychoanalysts have recognized the impossibility (and the undesirability) of a distant and authoritative approach. Instead, therapy is increasingly recognized as occurring precisely in the intersubjective dynamic between engaged patient and active, connected therapist. Only by becoming involved can a therapist offer a helpful intervention to a seeking patient.[2]

A new open, participatory approach characterizes a growing trend not only in psychoanalysis but also in the art of reading. Several branches of literary criticism (particularly postmodernism) insist that reading is not the passive receipt of an objective meaning. Instead, reading is understood to be the interaction of three players: the text, the reader, and the community in which the reader reads. All three have active roles to play in fixing what the text means to a specific person in a specific context. Meaning, then, emerges out of intersubjective involvement. Participation is everything.[3]

In scholarship, in medicine, in business, and in other fields, the mechanistic, objective model of the expert who stands above criticism and scrutiny or reproach is giving way to a new, more involved ideal. In religion, too, the distanced ideal is receding.[4] The rabbi and cantor of the past were often placed on a high podium ("six feet above criticism") from which they (actively) performed the worship service for a (passive) congregation. Rabbis, cantors, and educators generally did not make friends within their congregations; interaction was formal and controlled. We Jews have built beautiful sanctuaries and conducted majestic services, but Jewish authority figures sometimes infantilized our people and sterilized our faith. In our search for meaning, for values, and for warmth, the surprising miracle is that so many Jews still look to Judaism at all!

The Jewish community has begun to address the popular need for Jewish leaders who are willing to share their spiritual journeys, educate through consensus, and refrain from indiscriminately imposing their will. The architecture of new synagogues often reflects this openness: pulpits are much closer to the pews, the Torah is accessible to all, sanctuaries are laid out in the round. Yet these changes in style and popular expectations are only a beginning; we have yet to make the leap from the modernist ideal of leader as infallible source of authority to the traditional (and reemerging) vision of leader as model, participant, and guide.

Not surprisingly, this vision of leadership, this holistic understanding of teaching, turns out to be not so new after all. The very idea of Torah involves this rich symbiosis of learning and becoming:

> Of all the terms for God's instructions, none better characterizes Deuteronomy [than Torah], since it connotes both law and an instruction that must be taught, studied, and pondered, and it is expected to shape the character, attitudes, and conduct of those who do so. . . In later times, the term Torah was applied to the entire Pentateuch as "the Teaching" or "Instruction" par excellence.[5]

Indeed, the term Torah has come to connote the entire Jewish tradition, a veritable synonym for Judaism itself.[6] Notice that Torah isn't just what is given; it is what emerges from the dynamic of studying, pondering, and interpreting. Torah is content, but it is also process. The learning of Torah—shaping character, attitude, and conduct—integrates mind, heart, and soul.

In fact, this holistic approach, far from presenting a novelty, reaches all the way back to Moshe Rabbenu, Moses Our Rebbe, who lived among his people. The practice of communal living guided the rabbis of antiquity, who proceeded to live with their students. My rebbe, Rabbi Simon Greenberg of blessed memory, used to say, "If you think it's new, it probably isn't. And if it is new, it's probably wrong." This model of molding a *neshamah* (soul), of not just sharpening and informing a mind, has formed the core of Jewish pedagogy from the start. Among the tales of the great Talmudic mentor-rebbes, many are the stories involving their teaching outside a classroom or sanctuary, both through preaching and through caring social involvement. Hillel, for example, knew of a wealthy man who had lost all his money. Hillel provided for the man's needs, even maintaining a horse for him to ride and a servant to run before the horse. One day Hillel could not hire a servant, so he personally ran before the horse. His disciples were shocked, but Hillel explained that it was important to provide for each person's needs according to his accustomed standard. The great sage invoked the Torah and stressed that because each person reflects the divine image, maintaining another person's dignity is nothing less than the service of God.[7] To make the point crystal clear, Rabban Gamliel used to admonish newly appointed mentors, "Do you imagine that I offer you power? It is servitude that I offer you, as it is said, 'If you will be a servant to these people today and serve them' [1 Kings 12:7]."[8]

For thousands of years, Jewish civilization has treasured knowledge in the service of wisdom and has done so through teachers who shared their very lives with their students. As Rabbi Eugene Borowitz noted:

> Not the least aspect of being a community figure was serving as a role model. His disciples wanted to see how the master lived as well as to hear his teachings. And they then told their disciples what their masters did in the most diverse human situations. Their tales speak less of the sages as essentially sober, rational types, than of quite passionate men who regularly break into tears or otherwise give vent to their joy, distress or exasperation.[9]

The rebbe of the Talmud was a mentor who had a small circle of students. Those disciples lived with their mentor, worked with him, studied with him, and traveled with him. Not surprisingly, that intimacy created strong bonds of love between mentor and disciples. One of the greatest of the mentor-rebbes, Rabban Yoḥanan ben Zakai, praised his rebbe, Hillel, saying, "If all the heavens were parchment and all the trees were quills and all the seas were ink, it would still be impossible for me to write down even a small part of all that I learned from my teacher."[10]

A mentor-rebbe served as a role model for how a Jew ought to behave, how a Jewish life can be devoted to the service of God and to the lives of others. The ancient rebbe Shimon was known as *haTzedek* (the Righteous) not only because of his piety toward God but also because of his kindness to his fellow human beings.[11] Just like Shimon *haTzedek*, each mentor is the point through which the Sacred enters the mundane. Each rebbe embodies divine empathy and love.

The mentor-rebbes of antiquity were rarely value neutral. Instead, each mentor's influence was proportional to his ability to apply Jewish law (*halachah*) and Jewish values (*midot*) to the lives of his disciples and community. Although many of us may not be qualified to serve as authorities in Jewish law (and that aspect of being a rebbe may best be left in the hands of the rabbis, cantors, and other scholars of *halachah*), we can serve each other by offering the vital functions of a mentor: imparting the values that Judaism holds dear, making ourselves manifestations of God's love and concern, and presenting ourselves as models of seeking, learning Jews. Some may feel uncomfortable with all this talk about the need for mentors who love their students and break down the professional boundaries that have accumulated in the Western world. For many Jews, all this verbiage of souls and love may sound sentimental and forced, perhaps even downright un-Jewish! Before we proceed to describe how to become such a mentor, then, let's spend some time inquiring just how Jewish, and just how rabbinic, this warm, involved kind of role modeling is. Let's take a look at the Jewish roots of mentor leadership.

Moses: The Mentor's Mentor

Who is a mentor-rebbe? Traditionally, a rebbe is one so filled with God's teachings and commandments, a person who by living a public life of Torah study and mitzvah observance, by demonstrating compassionate leadership, and by offering sympathy, help, and affection inspires another person to be a mentor in turn. A mentor precisely blends the acts of knowing, doing, and caring.

The Torah is the central Jewish guide to leadership, and within the Torah the principal human figure is Moses. Jewish tradition instructs us, in the words of the Passover Haggadah, "In every generation, each person should see himself or herself as though personally freed from Egypt." Moses, after all, molds a stubborn group of slaves into a free people. Moses listens to our complaints, brings us to Mount Sinai, and leads us through forty years of wandering. Moses intervenes with God on our behalf and with us on God's behalf. Moses ushers us into our age-old Brit (Covenant) with God. Our Torah teaches, "Never again did there arise in Israel a prophet like Moses."[12] As a token of his unique status as leader, Moses is known as Moshe Rabbenu, Moses Our Rebbe.

The Torah portrays Moses as a man of extraordinary empathy and passion. Witnessing an Egyptian taskmaster beating a Hebrew slave, Moses is so enraged by the injustice that he instantly strikes down the taskmaster. Pharaoh's determination to execute Moses in retaliation for this "crime" forces Moses to flee to Midian, where he continues to identify with the weak and the outcast. Standing by a well, he witnesses a group of men harassing some shepherd women trying to water their flock. Once again Moses is incapable of indifference: "Moses rose to their defense, and he watered their flock."[13] Rabbinic tradition expands on this biblical portrayal of engaged empathy. According to the Midrash, Moses's rebuke of the men moves them to repent and to make way for the women's flocks. Then Moses "not only watered the women's flocks but also those of the shepherds, thus demonstrating that the way of admonition is through peace and friendly understanding."[14]

The women are so impressed with this courageous man that they inform their father, the priest Jethro, of Moses's action. Jethro in turn invites Moses to join them for a meal. Ultimately, Moses marries one of Jethro's daughters, Tziporah. Moses then enters a new stage of his life, as a shepherd. The job choice seems logical. After all, being a good shepherd isn't so different from being a mentor, is it? As one midrash (rabbinic interpretation of the Bible) notes: "Why did our ancestors choose to become shepherds? Because the tending of sheep afforded them opportunity to train themselves in compassion for all creatures."[15] Both callings, shepherding and mentoring, require constant vigilance of the well-being of those being supervised. Both muster the highest degree of intuition and attentiveness. And both require a willingness to exemplify compassion and leadership for those who would follow in one's path. While the Torah silently skips over Moses's youthful tenure as shepherd, rabbinic tradition recognizes it as the time when Moses demonstrated his fitness to lead God's people. One midrash states:

> Once, while Moses, Our Mentor, was tending Jethro's sheep, one of the sheep ran away. Moses ran after it until it reached a small, shaded place. There the lamb came across a pool of water and began to drink. As Moses approached the lamb, he said, "I did not know you ran away because you were thirsty. You are so exhausted!" He then put the lamb on his shoulders and carried him back. The Holy Blessing One said, "Since you tend the sheep of human beings with such overwhelming love—by your life, I swear you shall be the shepherd of my sheep—Israel."[16]

God singles out Moses's "overwhelming love" as integral in selecting him to lead the Israelites to freedom. Indeed, rabbinic tradition recognizes that same solicitousness in Moses's turning to look again at the wondrous burning bush: "Rabbi Isaac said, 'What is the meaning of the verse 'He turned to see'? The Holy Blessing One said, 'Moses

turned with anxiety, beholding the troubles of Israel in Egypt. Therefore is he worthy to become a shepherd and leader over them.'"[17]

Perhaps it is that extraordinary ability to love and nurture that
won Moses the most startling of biblical epithets: "nursing father."[18]
His devotion is so profound that the Torah compares his relationship
with the Jews to that of a mother with her suckling infant. Like a
mother with her children, Moses knows that his mentorship of the
Israelites requires tremendous resolve. One midrash even portrays
God warning Moses and Aaron of the difficulties of mentoring:

> The Holy Blessing One said to Moses and Aaron, "Know that my
> children are rebellious and troublesome. Therefore in accepting
> leadership over them you must be ready to listen even to their denun-
> ciations and to receive even their stones." This lesson should serve as
> a reminder to every leader and judge in Israel to exercise patience and
> forbearance when dealing with the people's problems.[19]

Another trait that makes Moses the ideal mentor is his eagerness
to see his flock rise to his level of leadership and vision. Some leaders
demand that power remain in their hands alone and that they retain
exclusive control over every decision. Not so with Moses: he is happy
to measure his success as a leader by his followers' growing ability to
lead themselves. In one biblical tale, Moses complains to God that the
responsibility of leading the Israelites is overwhelming, exclaiming,
"I cannot carry all this people by myself, for it is too much for me!"[20]
Moses knows intuitively that shared responsibility is better than even
the most efficient dictatorship. In response to Moses's cry, God instructs him to gather seventy elders and promises to "draw upon the
spirit that is on you and put it upon them; they shall share the burden
of the people with you, and you shall not bear it alone."[21]

Let's take a second biblical example: "Moses gathered the seventy
elders outside the Tent of Meeting. God descended in a cloud and
"drew upon the spirit that was on Moses and put it upon the seventy
elders. And when the spirit rested upon them, they spoke in ecstasy,
but did not continue."[22] With the descent of God's spirit, the elders

acquire the power of prophecy. Moses is delighted to be able to share his responsibilities and prerogatives with others. His willingness to share power is further highlighted by his response to the action of two men, Eldad and Meidad, who remain in the camp. When God's spirit descends on the other elders, Eldad and Meidad begin to prophesy right where they are. Joshua reports this to Moses, indignant that the honor of his mentor is somehow compromised. "My lord, Moses, restrain them!" he urges. Moses's response to his zealous aide reveals how deeply committed he is to shared leadership: "Are you wrought up on my account? Would that all of the Holy One's people were prophets, that the Holy One's spirit was upon them!"[23]

Humility is the finest fruit of Moses's special passion for his people and his God. According to biblical and rabbinic tradition, Moses is the most humble of God's servants. Eager to render glory to God, Moses would most likely have been delighted to know that the religion he midwifed does not bear his name, the location of his grave is unknown, and his name isn't so much as mentioned in the traditional telling of the Passover story.[24] Jewish tradition honors the greatness of Moses while insisting that his is a derivative glory: his access to God is due to the merit of the Jewish people. At the same time that Moses is at the top of Mount Sinai receiving God's Ten Commandments, the Israelites build the Golden Calf and begin their idolatrous celebration. God instructs Moses to "go down."[25] Rabbi Eliezer recognizes that to mean that "the Holy Blessing One said to Moses, 'Moses, descend from your greatness. Have I given you greatness except for the sake of Israel? And now Israel has sinned; so why do I want you?'"[26] A mentor's greatness is measured in part by the ability of his or her community to live an integrated, joyous, spiritual life. If the community fails at that task, the mentor has failed, too.

Moses is a mentor because his love for his people is at the core of his inspiration. That love and his humility readily translate into empathy, a desire to help, and an eagerness to raise the people to a point where each can embrace his or her spiritual birthright. So profound is Moses's commitment to his people that initially he refuses God's invitation to lead the Israelites because he is angry with God for abandoning the Jews for more than two hundred years and for allowing so many of them to die as slaves.[27] Moses speaks so harshly to God at the apparent delay in the liberation that Justice urges God to destroy Moses, "but after God saw that Moses argues this way only because of [his love for] Israel, God does not allow the Attribute of Justice to strike him."[28] With room for doubt, anger, and uncertainty, being a spiritual mentor begins with an existential commitment to the people around us and to God.

The Ancient Leaders: Mentors of the Talmud

With Moses's example at its core, there is little wonder that rabbinic Judaism nurtures the kind of intuitive leadership that relishes an empathetic and mutually enriching relationship between mentor and student. It is this intuition that makes Mentor Yoḥanan ben Zakai an exemplary rebbe-mentor. It is said of him, "No one but he ever opened the door for his students to enter."[29] Far from seeing himself as primarily interested in honing the skills of his younger colleagues, Rebbe Yoḥanan and the sages of the Talmud and the Midrash present themselves as eager to open their hearts and lives to those interested in growing in God's Covenant with the Jewish people. Their lives and challenges provide the best tools with which to encourage their students' journeys.

These ancient mentors were passionate in their devotion to God and their love of Torah. It is precisely because of that passion, the sources relate, that they refused to segregate Torah from wisdom or existence. Instead, they insisted that true Torah learning must translate into better living, that the book must infuse the life. Leadership for these sages involved soul transformation and social justice—the translation of details into insight and insight into action. "Rabbi Hiyya said, 'If someone studies Torah without the intention of fulfilling it, it would have been better never to have been born.' . . . Rabbi Aha said, 'One who learns in order to do is worthy to receive the *ruaḥ ha-Kodesh* [spirit of God].'"[30] The goal of the study of Torah is creating a soul, nurturing a heart, performing deeds of holiness and wholeness. Study provides a means, not an end. The context that lends meaning to study is again relationship—between the mentor and others, between the heritage and the disciple, between God and the seeking soul, between the world and humanity.

Relationships, like Torah, have both a cognitive and an emotional component. Rabbi Israel Salanter, the great nineteenth-century leader of the Musar movement, explained the biblical verse "Know, therefore, this day, and consider it in your heart"[31] to mean that "knowledge by itself is not sufficient; it must also penetrate into your heart."[32] Rabbi Meir realized that Jewish learning is nothing less than a life of beauty and balance. As the great sage Rava insisted, "The ultimate purpose of Torah wisdom is *teshuvah* [repentance] and good deeds. It makes no sense that a person should study the written and oral Torah and then kick his father or mother or mentor."[33] The vindication of Jewish learning is compassionate and ethical behavior, not merely the mastery of texts or the observance of ritual.

Time and again, these sages insisted that the essence of their rabbinic prowess rested on their moral example:

> Rabbi Elazar ben Shamua's students asked him, "To what do you attribute your longevity?" He replied, "I never walked in a fashion that implied that I was walking on the heads of the holy people." Rabbi Nehunia ben haKana's students said to him, "To what do you attribute your longevity?" He replied, "I never did anything that would bring me honor by humiliating someone else." Rabbi Zeira's students asked him, "To what do you attribute your longevity?" He replied, "I never lost my temper in my house, . . . and I never found pleasure in someone else's misfortune or failure."[34]

The transmission of information and skills may be possible in the lecture hall and the laboratory. However, the creation of decency and integrity requires far more time and subtlety. Mentor learning cannot be spoon-fed. Truth can never be fully verbalized, nor can it ever be made fully explicit. Instead, a mentor works to bring his or her disciples to the brink of insight, providing just enough tools (of knowledge, morality, and soul) to allow the partner to intuit the truth. The ancient mentor Hillel understood that need. A pagan once approached the great sage Shammai, telling him he desired to convert to Judaism so that he could wear the resplendent garments of the High Priest. Disdainful of this combination of ignorance and arrogance, Shammai pushed him away. The man then approached Hillel, expressing the same desire, and Hillel quietly began to spend time with the man, teaching him those sections of the Torah that pertained to the High Priest. When the man discovered that even King David was not allowed to encroach on the Holy of Holies and the terrain of the priests in the Temple in Jerusalem, the man realized that he could never become a *kohen*, much less the Kohen Gadol! Delighted to have gleaned this insight and grateful for Hillel's gift of time and caring, the man "appeared before Hillel and cried out, 'O patient Hillel! Blessings on your head because you have brought me under the wings of the Sh'chinah [the Divine Immanence]!'"[35] The gift of connection, of involvement, is the bottom line for such a rich harvest, and it is the primary tool of the mentor.

The great rabbis of the past learned by observation and imitation, as we saw in the poignant tale of Rav Kahana and his teacher (cited at the beginning of this chapter). An almost identical tale is recounted between yet another mentor and protégé, suggesting that this kind of transmission happens again and again in every mentor-disciple relationship:

> Rabbi Akiva said, "I once followed my teacher, Rabbi Yehoshua, into the bathroom and learned three things about personal care from

him." . . . Said Ben-Azai to Rabbi Akiva, "How could you dare to do such a thing with your mentor?" Said Rabbi Akiva to him, "This too is Torah, and I need to learn it."[36]

That same method has been a source of inspiration spanning the generations: we have already noted that Rabban Yoḥanan insisted on opening the door for his students. His example inspired younger mentors too: "As a result, his student Rabbi Eliezer acted in a similar fashion."[37]

We as students learn to become our truest selves by watching our mentors. Hence, the best way to teach morality and empathy is to embody them and cultivate a relationship with those who turn to us so that they will want to model our behavior. This transformation occurs through instruction—which is self-conscious and proceeds from mentor to protégé through emulation, which is also self-conscious but is offered by the protégé in response to the mentor—and through imitation, whether conscious or not, as the protégé walks the path of the mentor. There are no shortcuts in the building of character. The devotion of mentors must also extend beyond the walls of the classroom, the boardroom, and the sanctuary.

By now it should be clear that the mentor model of leadership encompasses far more than classroom management, inspirational sermons, efficient meetings, or behavior modification. Jewish tradition, both biblical and rabbinic, offers countless examples of great prophets and sages willing to nourish their disciples' minds, hearts, and souls by sharing their journey of Torah and life. The test of whether one has learned Torah is not revealed in a blue book, a task completed, or a successful event but in a life well lived. To empower others to live lives of goodness and *sh'leimut* (wholeness) requires more than skill (although it takes abundant skills) and knowledge (although rigorous knowledge is an essential base). To assist others in living full lives involves nothing less than devotion, love, and steadfastness. To be a mentor is to lead and transform through relationship.

The Mentors of the Past Still Lead Us Today

Jewish tradition recognizes that the primary way in which to learn goodness is to watch it. Disciples observe their mentors' behavior and then mimic it. In the process, they make the behavior their own. No number of lectures can distract a person from the reality of what mentors do. In the world of character formation, in the realm of values and leadership, we do what we see.

The examples of the mentors of the Talmud shine on in their stories, and they remind us of what is still possible for us. It is still possible for us to fashion opportunities for growth in which the bond between mentor and protégé is the central tool for transmitting Torah and inspiring a life of good deeds. We can still learn from the ancient sages that transformation goes on not only in executive committees but also in life's quieter moments, not only in the classroom but also in our private downtime. We can still learn that every encounter is an opportunity to teach Torah through our actions. The mentor-rebbes of antiquity remind us by their lives that a belief in God's love means nothing if we are not willing to shower that love on each other. They also demonstrate that the most resilient leaders are crafted and inspired in this caring way.

Because disciples develop similarly to children, Judaism has often compared mentors to parents: the sages of old apply to disciples the biblical verse "You shall teach them diligently to your children"[38] because "you find in so many instances that disciples are called children."[39] The next step, then, in our growth as mentors is to see what information on parenting we can glean from Jewish wisdom.

Leaders and Mentors in Today's World

Chapter Three

Parents: The Quintessential Mentors

When a parent guides sons and daughters in the right path, scripture says, "And you shall know that your tent is peace [Job 5:24]."

—YEVAMOT

Children mirror their parents' behavior. I remember once seeing my little daughter stand on her tiptoes, lean forward, look into a mirror, and poke herself in the eye. I realized that these were indeed the actions that my wife performed when she put on her contact lenses each morning. I recall, too, the first Shabbat on which my son, at age two and a half, walked up and down the aisles of my congregation's sanctuary and shook everyone's hand, saying, "Shabbat shalom." I understood that he was imitating the way his *Abba* greeted the congregants week after week. As the Talmud explains, "What the child says in the street comes from the father or the mother."[1] Thus we come to realize that a child's first teachers, those who can never be replaced, are the parents.

Talmud Torah (education) is of course about training the intellect, but it is also about instilling values, building character, and cultivating wonder. One of our most valued goals in education is learning *menschlichkeit,* the idea, conveyed by that splendid Yiddish word, of being the best one can be. To be a mensch is a lifelong journey involving every aspect of our being: our intellect, our knowledge, our relationships, our very souls. As the Bible well understands, *"Yirat HASHEM reishit da'at"* (Awe of God is the beginning of knowledge).[2]

Parents are the first and most important mentors because long before intellectual training begins, children are able to absorb lessons of curiosity and caring, of empathy and thoughtfulness.[3] Parents are the ones who respond to their children's first ideas, feelings, dilemmas. The hardest questions, those that have perplexed philosophers and theologians across the ages, are often found on the lips of little children. And it is their parents who have the immediate opportunity to respond to the questions "Why?" "Says who?" and "How?" Even if they may not have the complete or final answers, parents are the ones the child watches; they are each person's first teacher and mentor.

Parents as Mentors

Like all guides, parents introduce their children to the realities of life and how to respond to them. Sometimes they do it intentionally, and sometimes the awareness erupts despite their best intentions.

A young father recounted to me that once while he was walking to services with his daughter, then four years old, she asked him if Pocahontas was still alive.

"No," he told her, "Pocahontas lived a long time ago."

Emily, the daughter, considered this answer for a moment and then asked, "Dad, people who lived a long time ago died a long time ago, right?"

"Right."

"And we are living now. Does that mean we will die now?"

Emily's father assured her that they would live a long, long time. She asked him if he would live until she got married, and he told her that he would live even longer, until she had children of her own. Again Emily fell silent, and then she said, "Dad, when you die, I will hold your hand and die with you."

"No, sweetheart," he said. "When I die, I want you to keep living for a long time."

"Why, Dad?"

"Because you're my little girl, and I want you to live."

She was again quiet for a moment, and then he heard a sniffle, which grew into a sob.

"Emily! Why are you crying?" he asked.

"Because I don't want to live if you aren't living."

He hugged his little girl, telling her that he would always be with her, that he would always be in her heart, that he wouldn't die until she was very, very old. At that point, his words and actions as a father weren't much different from the wise words and actions of any mentor. Mentors act like parents to their disciples, and parents act like mentors to their children.

Rabbinic legend tells us, too, that it is from their parents that children learn of the world. We are told that all children know supernatural truths—a heavenly Torah—while still in the womb.[4] At the moment of birth, an angel strikes the child above the lips, creating a dent and causing the child to forget all the Torah he or she ever knew. As children begin their residence on earth, they are open and fresh, ready to reclaim the cosmic teaching they used to know, doing so by mimicking the Torah of their parents' lives and love.

Just as the Torah addresses itself to every subject under the sun, so the parents, the child's first mentors, introduce the child to every matter that will be needed later in life. Getting along with others, the physical properties of the world, songs, values, and a sense of identity—all are part of the vast array of knowledge and wisdom that parenting should bestow on children. And children are interested not only in mechanics but even more in meaning. As the parent of any young child will attest, the most frequent question asked is not "How" but "Why?" Why should we do this and not that? Why should we act this way and not that way? Why does the world work this way? Why? Why? Why?

Sometimes an answer fails to resolve a problem but at least provides a way to cope and endure. When he was seventy-five, Jack, a businessman, told of the time when as a young child he awoke in the middle of the night to the sound of sirens, fire trucks, and screams. A house across the street was burning, and the street was in turmoil. Terrified, Jack shouted for his mother, who ran to his room. He sought assurances that such a thing couldn't happen to him, that he wouldn't be hurt, but his mother would offer no guarantees. Instead, she told him to lay his head on his pillow, close his eyes, and recite the Sh'ma. He did and was comforted. To this day, well more than half a century later, Jack recites the Sh'ma whenever he feels overwhelmed or afraid. And he is still comforted by the sense of God's presence, and his mother's. Providing a Jewish way to respond to life's challenges and life's joys is a gift that can last a lifetime, whether it comes from a parent or a teacher.

Because children learn through observing and imitating, how we live our lives constitutes their first core curriculum. Not only through our words alone but also through our actions do they learn what is right, acceptable, and good. That learning goes on all day every day, during meals, during baths, during playtime. Infants don't sit in a classroom reading their parents' words; they imbibe their family's values during meals, baths, and play.

Consider a special moment in just about any synagogue service, a moment that cannot fail to inspire with its simplicity. It does not involve the cantor's chants or the rabbi's sermon. It's not even found in the Torah. But it happens almost weekly: a toddler drops a prayer book during services. After all, to the child the book feels immense, far too big and heavy for little hands to hold. But the child wants to mimic what he or she sees the parents doing and so insists on holding the book. And then comes the magic, the silent act of the mentor: Mom or Dad bends down, picks up the book, and kisses it before handing it back to the child. No lecture. No instruction. Just a parent showing a child how to revere a special book. And almost every time, the child's response is to kiss the book too.

Parents are open books before their children, for the children are always watching, always listening, always learning. For that reason, it is crucial for parents to share their thoughts, ideals, and values with their children. So, too, as mentors we must be open before those who seek our guidance. We must share every response, every concern, every joy, and every sorrow. This holistic teaching is what being a mentor is all about: it transcends the text by using a growing base of knowledge of the Torah to refine the teaching of ethics, priorities, and character.[5] A midrash comments on the proverb "Train up a child in the way the child should go"[6] by noting that "this means that if you train your child with words of Torah until the child matures, the child will remain loyal to them."[7] As parents and as parent-like mentors, we are involved in nothing less than cultivating someone's very humanity. Yet like all great mentors, parents have two powerful tools at their disposal: God's Torah and their personality.

A Word About Torah…and Teenagers

In contemporary life, the teen years are often marked by a growing separation from the parents as the children begin to explore their identity as separate from that of their parents. Jewish families aren't exempt from the social pressures that can divide parents and teenagers, but a home that comes together around a Sabbath table or in celebration of a Jewish holy day or festival, or one that has integrated the values of Torah, can find the common ground that will help them bridge that gap.

For parents, one of the joys of living in California is getting to choose when to introduce their children to the phenomenon of snow. When the children of a friend of mine reached the ripe ages of fifteen and sixteen, my friend and his wife decided that the time had arrived. They packed their van and took off for a weekend at Lake Arrowhead (on the way to Palm Springs, about two hours outside Los Angeles), which is about five thousand feet above sea level and a world away from suburbia.

Once they were well on our way, Stacey, my friend's daughter, asked her father to turn on the radio and told him which station she preferred. It was a contemporary rock station, and like untold generations of parents before him, he hated his child's music—the sound and the questionable values conveyed by the lyrics. The two began to quarrel about the songs, he insisting that they were degrading and she insisting that her father was too rigid, too judgmental, "too out of it." On the secular side, the difference between her generation and his seemed irreconcilable.

A few more miles down the road, my friend's wife and son had fallen asleep, leaving Stacey and her father alone to talk. Stacey began the conversation by informing him that the boys in her class played a fantasy game in which they pretended to be kings. After explaining that playing such a game might be a male trait (one that is present well into adulthood), he asked Stacey if she would want to be a monarch.

"Yes," she said, "wouldn't you?"

"No," he told her. "A king has to be in public all the time. A king has to attend endless banquets and never gets to just relax."

"Well," she informed him, "I would like to have a king's money."

Bracing himself for an expression of the rampant materialism he expected would follow, he asked Stacey, "What would you do with a king's money if you had it?"

And here's where the miracle of the values of Torah broke through their generation gap. Stacey said, "Dad, if I had a king's money, I'd give it to *tzedakah*. I'd build lots of shuls and lots of schools. And I'd make sure that poor people had enough to eat every day." She paused and then added, "And I'd save enough to build myself a swimming pool."

Superficial father-daughter barriers disintegrated with the introduction of a shared set of values and love of Torah. Because both father and daughter try to translate the lofty values of Torah into the prosaic details of their lives, both speak the same language when it comes to what they expect of themselves and how they treat others.

They recognize their place in the world and know that no matter where they are, they are united in a bond more powerful than space and more timeless than their taste in music. Through the prism of Torah, they talk the same talk.

There is no greater antidote to the generation gap than making the study and application of Torah the center of Jewish life, both for the family and for the community. Perhaps this is the reality that the prophet recognized when he foretold, "God will turn the parents to their children and the children to their parents."[8] The venue from which Torah can shine remains the human heart. Both adults and children are able to absorb the lesson of Torah. However, the tools that transmit these lessons are our character and our experiences—in sum, our personality.

The Tool of Personality

The greatest teaching tools that we as mentors possess are our humor, our habits, and our humanity. Teaching through the lens of one's character and experiences finds consummate expression in this story from the Talmud: A wealthy man inserted an odd provision into his will, insisting that his son inherit nothing until he was willing to act like a fool in public. What could such an odd stipulation mean? And would it invalidate the will according to Jewish law? To discover the answer to the legal question, a delegation of rabbis went to consult Rabbi Yehoshua ben Korhah, one of the greatest rabbinic authorities of his time.

> When they peeked in from outside [his house], they saw him crawling on his hands and knees, with a reed sticking out of his mouth, being pulled along by his child. Seeing him thus, they discreetly withdrew, but they came back later and asked him about the provision in the will. Rabbi Yehoshua ben Korhah laughed and said, "As you live, this business you ask about—acting the fool—was precisely what happened to me a few moments ago!"[9]

Here we have a mentor story within a mentor story! Rabbi Yehoshua is willing to share every part of his personality with his children; the great sage is not above getting on the floor and acting like a donkey so that his children can laugh and play with him. And like all instances of play, this one conveys serious ideas just under the surface: about leadership, about work, and about connection. But Rabbi Yehoshua isn't just a teacher to his children; he is a mentor to his colleagues as well. He willingly shares the truth about his donkey games with his fellow rabbis. On the deepest level, Rabbi Yehoshua shows his colleagues that being a great mentor summons the same skills as being a great father. He reveals more than a provision in the will, not only showing what involved fathering is all about, not only offering his playfulness as a way to nurture his children, but also ultimately integrating into his life a way to be a role model to adults. As a mentor and as a parent, he exposed and offered all his gifts simultaneously. This wonderful father and mentor used his personality as a tool, guiding his children and his colleagues to an understanding of important lessons of character and identity by offering the full range of his emotions and making himself vulnerable.

The Gift of Presence

Of course, sharing one's personality takes time, and the gift of presence is the prerequisite for internalizing a mentor's strength of character, wisdom, and resilience. As with the tool of personality, the gift of time—of presence—is amply illuminated in the world of parenting: parents lavish countless hours on their children, from infancy to adolescence. The very fact that time is spent with the child offers the child a resilient sense of worth, thereby providing a firm base on which to stand for the rest of his or her life.

A Talmudic example comes to mind:

Every Friday afternoon, Rabbi Yehoshua regularly listened to his grandson's reading of the weekly Torah lesson. Once he forgot to do so, and, when he had already entered the baths of Tiberias . . . he remembered that he had not listened to his grandson. So he turned around and left. Rabbi Hiyya bar Abba asked him, "Mentor, did you not teach us that one may not interrupt if one has already begun [to bathe]?" Rabbi Yehoshua answered, "Hiyya, my son, is it a small matter to you that one who listens to his grandson's reading of Torah is as though he were hearing it at Mount Sinai? For it is said, 'Make them known to your children and your children's children, as if it were the day that you stood before the Holy One your God in Horeb' [Deuteronomy 4:9–10]."[10]

Rabbi Yehoshua's practice of listening as his young grandson recite what he had learned about the weekly Torah portion offers a model of time and presence. Picture how proud the child would have been able to study Torah with his learned grandfather! What delight the two must have derived from sharing that time together!

With these stories, we see the way in which being a parent (or grandparent) encompasses being a mentor to a child, just as being a mentor springs from a willingness to parent others. Rabbi Yehoshua refers to his student, Rabbi Hiyya, as his son and explains that it is permissible to deviate from normal legal practice (not to interrupt a bath once begun) for the sake of hearing one's grandchild recite Torah. In fact, the very portrayal of a great mentor taking a bath with his disciple is one of great intimacy! But we intrude on their privacy in the service of the human side of Torah, waiving a procedural rule for a chance to observe the demonstration of a more important value: generations linked in the timeless unfolding of Torah.

Rabbi Yehoshua is willing to use the tool of his personality to educate both his grandson and his younger colleague. He is also aware that such a tool requires consistent commitment in order to be effective. So he refuses to skip a session with this expectant grandson. Transformation and growth take time, as we see expressed in an often-quoted passage in the book of Psalms: "Your children shall be like olive saplings around your table,"[11] which Rabbi David Blumenthal elaborates to mean that "love as a virtue is an ongoing pattern. It is a commitment to plant, to weed, to water, to prune, and to harvest."[12]

Tzimtzum: Withdrawing to Make Room for Growth

Good parenting, like effective mentoring, requires the gifts of time and personality. But these tools are just the beginning. What we *do* with them makes all the difference, and the doing requires encouragement.

Ever since my son, Jacob, was an infant, I have read a story with him each night and then tucked him in, making sure the required stuffed animals are in their desired positions, that his red blanket is tucked under his arms, and that his pillow is fluffed under his head. Then, in the dark, Jacob and I take a moment to recite the Sh'ma together. Night after night through the years, we have shared this moment of quiet holiness. Those untold minutes, adding up to hours, came to a kind of fruition when Jacob's special-needs program, *Sha'arei Tikvah,* led Friday-night services at Valley Beth Shalom, a congregation in Encino, California. With hundreds of people present, Jacob went to the front of the sanctuary, climbed up the steep steps to the podium, covered his eyes, and belted out the Sh'ma. When he finished, he looked around the room with an enormous grin on his face. I think he was almost as surprised as the rest of us (and he was certainly as pleased). For a moment there was silence, and then the congregation burst into applause for him, which only compounded his delight. For the rest of the evening, whenever I mentioned his leading the Sh'ma, Jacob grinned.

Children look to their parents and other adults for encouragement, commitment, and love, offerings that can help a child to develop a happy, open personality. I recall the funeral of a former president of a Jewish Federation. In the chapel, one of his children delivered a eulogy, speaking about how her father's unfailing confidence in her had allowed her to succeed as a professional and as a wife. After the service, a former member of the Federation's board of trustees told her that her father had shown those same traits in his service with the other Federation volunteers, thereby raising a generation of Jewish leaders who also felt inspired to succeed.

Essential to the content of any parent-child interaction is the underlying message of love and connection. Even when a parent disapproves of what a child *does,* the criticism should never eclipse the fundamental approval of who the child *is.* Of course, good parenting (and good mentoring) requires appropriate criticism. But even critical comments must be constructive and supportive.

As a teenager, I often borrowed my stepfather's car. One day, driving a bit recklessly, I dented the side of the automobile. I was terrified when I imagined how my stepfather might respond, but when I confessed, he merely said, "Weren't there already some dents in it?" I have never forgotten that response, which taught me that in his eyes I was more important than any automobile.

No less important than showing love when offering criticism, good parenting involves making a space for the less-experienced child to understand the reasons for a rule or practice, with the goal of helping that child internalize the rules. The Jewish paradigm here is found in kabbalah, Jewish mysticism. According to the Lurianic account of Creation,[13] God is everywhere and pervades all. In order to create the cosmos, a space had to develop in which God did not exist, so that it could be filled with this new Creation. God's self-contraction, restraint, withdrawal *(tzimtzum)* created a hollow space in which matter, space, and time—the material cosmos—could be formed.

So, too, with mentoring: a mentor has to back off, creating enough space for a protégé to develop into that beckoning potential. This mode of being a mentor relies less on imposed rules and more on allowing the seeking soul to discover the law etched within. Rabbi Isaiah Horowitz, a great early-seventeenth-century kabbalist and authority on Jewish law, insisted that "when one wants something from the family, it is not proper to force them against their will. . . . Rather, try to persuade them as much as possible to want to do it of their own volition, for that is better than forcing them to do it."[14]

Rabbi Horowitz insisted that it is preferable to enlist consent. Enabling a child (or an acquaintance) to understand why something is permitted or prohibited, why we behave this way and not that way, conveys a message of trust essential to the child's (or the acquaintance's) sense of self-esteem. By engaging the other in the process of understanding and decision making, parents and mentors stimulate the ability of child, colleague, or student to make moral choices and shoulder responsibility. Mentors cannot replace the other's role in acquiring wisdom and becoming a leader. A mentor can guide, but it is the developing protégé who must fashion an identity and want to claim a leadership position.

Recognizing that the role of the mentor is not to spoon-feed a predigested truth but to bring the protégé to the brink of his or her potential is the key challenge facing any mentor. The *tzimtzum* of the mentor is to refrain from imposing a solution or articulating an answer. No less an authority than Maimonides offered that insight in his magisterial *Guide of the Perplexed*. Rambam recognized that "the subject matter will appear, flash, and then be hidden again."[15] The truths that can transform lives and build character are generally beyond verbalization; the gift a mentor can give is to assist the other in reaching the beginning of understanding and trusting the mind and heart so that he or she can cross the finish line independently. Ramban also said, "At the outset the intellect is incapable of receiving them [true opinions]; only flashes of them are made to appear so that the perfect person should know them."[16] What the mentor can do is prepare, trust, and step back.

Once during my high-school years, I faced one of those reoccurring dilemmas in which I had to choose between doing what I was supposed to do and doing what I wanted to do. My elderly grandmother had asked that I visit her. At the same time, a group of friends was going to the park to play ball. I wanted to be with my friends even though I loved my grandmother and knew how much my visit would mean to her. I felt torn between an intense desire to hang out with my peers and a sense of love and loyalty to my aged grandmother. I went to my mother, expecting that she would simply instruct me to visit my grandmother. Instead she responded, "Do what you think is best. You know what to do." By refusing to make the choice for me, my mother forced me to take responsibility for my behavior. That act of *tzimtzum,* of withdrawing, left a space that had previously been filled by her power as a parent. By leaving the space empty, she invited me to fill it with my ability to care for others and in doing so take a giant step toward adulthood. She demonstrated that my obligations were no longer a burden imposed by her, they were an expression of my integrity.

In the words of Rabbi Menachem Mendl, the Kotzker mentor, one of the greatest Ḥasidic sages, "You have two choices. You can force your children to study Torah, and they in turn will grow and force their children to do the same. Or you can devote some of your own time to your own Torah study. If you do the latter, you will find your children learning by your side."[17]

The Kotzker well understood the vital role of *tzimtzum* and the difference between lecturing and exemplifying. Coercion can compel behavior, but it cannot hope to win the heart or influence choices. A parent who forces a child to act teaches the child that the act is intrinsically undesirable. But parents who choose, for example, to study Torah in the presence of their children show the children that Torah study is a wonderful use of an adult's time. By withdrawing from an authoritarian role and making space by offering our behavior as an example, we make it possible for children and all those whose lives we touch to grow in the love of what we ourselves cherish.

The model of *tzimtzum* also holds out the reminder that making space in which a child or protégé can cultivate independence means that there are circumstances in which it is not possible for a mentor or a parent to determine the child's or protégé's choice of behavior. In such moments, responsibility or accountability belong to the protégé or child alone and cannot properly be shifted to parents or mentors. Parenting and mentoring are two-way streets: the parent and mentor must be willing to teach, and the child and protégé must be open to the teaching.

When the children of Israel gathered around the foot of Mount Sinai, the miracle was not only that God was willing to give the Torah. An equally great miracle was that the children of Israel were willing to receive it. Midrash enshrines that moment by commenting that the biblical phrase "We will do and we will hear" suggests a willingness to act on the Torah prior to examining its contents. So, too, offering our children or our protégés access to our experience, wisdom, or suggestions requires their willingness to listen.

The Dynamic of Honoring Parents—and Children

The importance of parents to children is codified in the fifth of the Ten Commandments: "Honor your father and your mother."[18] Indeed, the rabbis of the Talmud were so taken by the commandment's importance that they equated the honor due parents with the honor due God: "When people honor their father and mother, the Holy Blessing One says, 'I consider it as if I have lived among them and they had honored me.'"[19]

Yet honoring parents may be emphasized so strongly precisely because it is such a difficult mitzvah to observe and one that is so easily, so suddenly, transgressed. Not all parents make it easy, and some seem less deserving than others. A seemingly one-sided mitzvah (nowhere does the Torah mandate honoring children), this is one of those commandments whose apparent simplicity gives way to deeper complexity.[20]

The great rabbi Abraham Joshua Heschel wrote, "The problem I as a father face, is why my child should revere me. Unless my child will sense in my personal existence acts and attitudes that evoke reverence—the ability to delay satisfactions, to overcome prejudices, to sense the holy, to strive for the noble—why should he/she revere me?"[21] Parents have it in their power to make it possible for their children to fulfill this mitzvah wholeheartedly, yet they also have it in their power to make it virtually impossible for their children to fulfill this mitzvah without tearing a hole in their—their children's—heart. Parents who have abused their children, who have neglected them, or who have withheld affection are not easy to honor. Such parents put their children in the position of having to squelch their integrity or turn their back on this biblical mitzvah. As the medieval mystics insisted, "Parents must not so exasperate a child that the child cannot withstand rebelling against them."[22]

Because the parents shape the background of their child's fulfillment of the mitzvah, it might be more helpful to see this mitzvah as a *dynamic* linking parent and child in a context that both create together. In truth, parents must earn the honor of their children, and children must grow to recognize how much their parents have done to deserve the honor due them.

For the parents, the process of raising children is in part a burden. Parents may look to their children to fill the emotional deficits of their own childhood. Faced with the challenges of earning a livelihood and attending to the chores of daily life, it can become difficult to provide the steady love and approval children deserve. As the Midrash acknowledges, "It is easier to see a whole forest of young olive trees mature than to rear a single child."[23]

From the children's perspectives, it's hard to recognize how much work goes into being a parent. Focused on their own needs and growth, children don't often see their parents as human beings with shortcomings and foibles like anyone else. More often than not, children feel the brunt of frustrations their parents endure elsewhere. Again, the Midrash speaks to the heart in observing, "It is typical of human beings that anger in one's home rests on the littlest member."[24] With less experience and with their dependence on their parents so total (as to be frightening to the children), it is often impossible for children to comprehend their parents' behavior. Honoring one's parents poses a formidable challenge indeed.

So the ability to observe the commandment of honoring mother and father requires the active participation of both parents and children. Here, too, as with so many mitzvot, the proper context is within a relationship—there is a *brit* (a covenant) linking parent and child. And it is only within such a *brit* that honor can be expressed with sincerity.

As with parenting, the art of serving as someone's mentor requires making it possible for the each person in the relationship to want to learn by example. As a mentor, one accepts the obligation to behave in a way that facilitates relating, empathy, and growth. Just as there is a commandment to honor one's parents, so, too, is there one to honor one's mentors. Just as the mitzvah of *kibud av v'em* (honoring parents) presumes the dynamic give and take of commitment and love, so, too, does the relationship between teacher and student, clergy and congregant, leaders and members of a community.

Learning from One's Children

Actually, it's not enough to act in such a way as to be worthy of respect. Deserving honor requires a willingness to learn from one's children, students, congregants, or colleagues. Perhaps it is for this reason that the Talmud records the insight of one great sage: "Much Torah have I learned from my teachers, even more from my colleagues, and from my students, most of all."[25] Sometimes we learn life's most important lessons through the teachings of children. For example, I don't think I truly understood my message or felt the full power of the seventh day until my son, Jacob, who is autistic, gave me the gift of the Shabbat when he was six years old.

Newly living in Los Angeles and no longer leading a congregation, I looked forward to savoring the early-Shabbat-morning walk to our

synagogue with my son. On our first Shabbat, I tried to walk the way
most people walk. I wanted to arrive punctually. Jacob, on the other
hand, was already where he wanted to be: enjoying a walk with his
father. I cajoled, pulled, pushed, yelled, but Jacob would not rush.
Nothing worked. By the time we arrived at the synagogue, hopelessly
late, I was drenched in sweat and far too frustrated to pray. The second week repeated the aggravation of the first. We still reached services late, and I was so annoyed that I couldn't even sit still when we
did get to the sanctuary. The third week, I realized that Jacob wasn't
going to stop being Jacob, which meant that our walk would have to
proceed his way, on his schedule. I would have to abandon any commitment to schedule or pace.

As Jacob and I set out on walk number three, I tried paying no attention to our speed or direction. When I got to the corner, I didn't let
myself look at the traffic light—invariably green—until right before
Jacob caught up. Instead, I waited. From time to time, I turned just to
relish my son's meandering and found that his joy was contagious and
pure. Occasionally I found myself experiencing my old apprehen-
sions, worrying about what part of the service I was missing or how
we were not proceeding quickly enough. But the allure of the walk,
the sun, and my son restored me. Jacob's spirit had infected me.

When we finally arrived at the synagogue, the service was more
than half over. The worshipers were already returning the Torah Scroll
to the Ark. Jacob squealed with delight—"The Torah! The Torah!"—
and ran to the front of the sanctuary. Too excited to stand still, he
bounced on his toes next to the person holding the Scroll while the
congregation recited the ancient praise: *"Hodo al eretz v'shamayim!"*
(God's glory encompasses heaven and earth!) Jacob had showed me
how to see that glory, and he had taught me through his example that
we can't possibly be late because wherever we are, we are already
where we are supposed to be. Children, students, congregants—all of
them teach us great lessons if we are only open to receiving them.

What Can Mentors Learn from Parents

Being a mentor requires many of the same skills as being a parent. As the Midrash says, "Just as disciples are called children, so the teacher is called a parent."[26] Good parents use their personality as a tool to help their children make sense of the world. By sharing their reactions, humor, interests, and warmth, parents help children cherish and cultivate these rich gifts in themselves. And by spending a lot of time with their children, parents ensure enough safe supervision for children to explore the full extent of their own personalities, to test limits, and to find their own way.

Good parenting entails mentoring one's children. Being a good mentor involves parenting someone else's child. Serving as a mentor and being a parent are ways of sharing love and shaping lives. As similar as the roles are, being a mentor also involves a step beyond parenting. Any mentor is also a transitional figure, one who allows an individual to shift from exclusive reliance on the parents to a gradual recognition that other people can assist in the process of developing spiritual fulfillment and Jewish passion. As children begin to differentiate between themselves and their parents, evolving their unique identity, these additional caring adults can help smooth their path and keep them connected to a nexus of values, community, and identity. The mentor is part of a team, a link in the chain that connects each Jewish individual to community, heritage, and faith. There are times when parents cannot assist; there are places where parents cannot go. In such times and places, mentors can fill a void, helping each protégé know that he or she is loved and precious still.

Good parenting requires a willingness to share feelings, to commit one's self unconditionally, to connect, and to trust. Blessed are the children whose parents can provide those gifts consistently and abundantly. And happy are the parents who see their children grow in security, compassion, and wisdom because of the safety and example they provide.

Working is another way of praying.
You plant in Israel the soul of a tree.
You plant in the desert the spirit of gardens.

Praying is another way of singing.
You plant in the tree the soul of lemons.
You plant in the gardens the spirits of roses.

Singing is another way of loving.
You plant in the lemons the spirit of your son.
You plant in the roses the soul of your daughter.

Loving is another way of living.
You plant in your daughter the spirit of Israel.
You plant in your son the soul of the desert.[27]

Becoming a mentor involves a good deal of skill. But that skill rests on a foundation very similar to that required for sound parenting. A mentor is someone willing to serve a seeking Jew as a second parent. By offering our protégés—of any age—the tool of our personality and the gift of our presence, we stand in relation to them as parents do in relation to their children. And as parents do with their children, we can provide the warmth and security that allow the other to flourish and to bloom.

Chapter Four

Other Mentors

Come with me and gain knowledge of the Torah, that you may gain life in this world and in the Coming World.

—HILLEL, AVOT DE–MENTOR NATAN

Our parents shape our souls, guiding us on our journey through life. Formative as the role of our parents may be, many other people also make crucial contributions. It may well be that the blending of personality, presence, and time is precisely why learning from another is so crucial for human wholeness and community. Rabbinic tradition records that "a person who studies alone is no match for one who studies with a teacher,"[1] because insights are most profoundly transmitted from person to person. Spouses, friends, teachers, employers, colleagues, children, neighbors—all have served as mentors at one time or another. Indeed, we often act as mentors (intentionally or not) to those with whom we live and/or work. Just as good parents have much to pass on to us about how to act as soul mentors, so, too, do the many people who have offered us insight, courage, and counsel through our lives have much to teach us about mentoring. We all have the opportunity to learn from others with more experience, deeper insight, or other backgrounds. And we, in turn, have the opportunity to pass along life's lessons to other seeking souls. In this chapter, we'll look at some of the roles through which we can cultivate the souls of those we love, helping them to achieve wisdom, contentment, and wholeness.

Spouses

Adulthood is in part a reflection of the strengths and weaknesses of our childhood, yet—like childhood—it is also a time of growth. With each day, there are insights to make, challenges to master, and sensitivities to cultivate. We fashion ourselves anew at every step of our journey. And in that dynamic process of growth and transformation, we rely on those around us to guide us, correct us when we blunder, and commend us when we deserve praise.

In adult life, no one plays the important role of mentor and guide more than one's spouse. Preeminent among our most intimate family relations, one chooses to be a husband or wife. Children remain their parents' children no matter what the children do (or don't do), and a parent is forever, but a spouse is a spouse only so long as both partners cherish their mutual commitment—ideally, one that is based on love, trust, and a shared destiny. A relationship with a spouse is both a paradigm and an intensification of all other relationships.

But what makes a spouse a mentor? In a relationship that is strong and healthy, a spouse is able to criticize and disagree as an act of loyalty and love. Even during disagreements, the recognition that both partners are ultimately on the same side, struggling together to achieve a resolution that is beneficial to both of them forms the precious gift that only a spouse can give. In a strong marriage, a spouse can instruct and uplift his or her partner even during life's most difficult trials. For example, a precious bond existed between the tannaitic sage Rabbi Meir and his wife, Beruriah, the couple presented in rabbinic literature as a remarkable pair—both learned in Torah, both pious, both loyal to those they love. A midrash explains the proverb "What a rare find is a capable wife"[2] by showing us the mentoring wisdom and courage of Beruriah:

It happened that while Rabbi Meir was expounding in the house of study on a Sabbath afternoon his two sons died. What did their mother do? She put them both on a couch and spread a sheet over them.

At the end of the Sabbath, Rabbi Meir returned home from the house of study and asked, "Where are my two sons?" She replied, "They went to the house of study." Rabbi Meir: "I looked for them there but did not see them." Then she gave him the cup for *havdalah*, and he pronounced the blessing. Again he asked, "Where are my two sons?" She replied, "They went to such and such a place and will be back soon." Then she brought food for him.

After he had eaten, she said, "My teacher, I have a question." Rabbi Meir: "Ask your question." She: "My teacher, a while ago a man came and deposited something in my keeping. Now he has come back to claim what he left. Shall I return it to him or not?" Rabbi Meir: "My daughter, is not one who holds a deposit required to return it to its owner?" She: "Still, without your opinion, I would not have returned it."

Then what did she do? She took Rabbi Meir by his hand, led him up to the chamber, and brought him near the couch. Then she pulled off the sheet that covered them, and he saw that both children lying on the couch were dead. He began to weep and say, "My sons, my sons, my teachers, my teachers. My sons in the way of the world, but my teachers because they illumined my eyes with their understanding of Torah." Then she came out with "My teacher, did you not say to me that we are required to restore to the owner what is left with us in trust? 'The Lord has given, and the Lord has taken away. May the Name of the Lord be blessed' [Job 1:21]." Rabbi Ḥanina said, "In this manner she comforted him and brought him solace; hence it is said, 'What a rare find is a capable wife!'"[3]

How fitting that it is a wife, a woman intimately aware of her power as a spouse, who shows us how to be a mentor. She uses her husband's love of Torah and their love for each other to help her husband cope with what is surely one of life's greatest agonies.

A courageous spouse is essential not only when we must face life's sorrows but also when we must own up to our shortcomings—as the following story illustrates. Just after a colleague's child was born, a congregant whom my fellow rabbi holds dear commented that the baby looked no different to him than a carp. The rabbi was stung by the remark. The next morning just before services began, the man pulled the rabbi aside to apologize. "Rabbi," he said, "last night I told Sandy what I had said about your kid, and she practically threw me out. I know I hurt your feelings, and I'm sorry." The congregant's wife knew that her relationship with her husband was strong enough that he would listen to her criticism. And she loved her husband enough to tell him what he needed to hear even if he didn't necessarily want to hear it. She helped him restore an important relationship and experience the power inherent in the act of apologizing.

That gift of soul is one that can emerge only within a context of love and shared destiny, and no one embodies that connection and commitment as much as a spouse. Perhaps that is why the great sages of the Talmud equated a good marriage with nothing less than the presence of God: "The Divine Presence [the name Yah] is the link between husband and a wife: the *yud* in *ish* [husband] and the *hay* in *ishah* [wife]. If they are worthy, the Presence abides between them, and they are blessed."[4]

In times of error, a spouse can chastise in the spirit of the Bible itself, which defines *tochahah* (rebuke) as an act of devotion and fidelity: "You shall not hate your kinsfolk in your heart. Reprove your kinsman but incur no guilt because of him. . . . Love your fellow as yourself; I am the Holy One."[5]

The Torah understands that constructive rebuke can occur only within the context of connection and love. Without that background, such criticism can be destructive and malicious. But within a loving commitment, it takes empathy, devotion, and courage to tell your beloved that he or she can do better. Because of the unique commitment that spouses make to each other, because of how well one spouse gets to know the other, because only a spouse sees the fullness of one's personality and character, a spouse is uniquely qualified and positioned to deliver *tochahah*. Such a commitment is illustrated in yet another story about Rabbi Meir and Beruriah:

In the neighborhood of Rabbi Meir there lived hooligans, who annoyed him so much that he prayed for them to die. His wife, Beruriah, said to him: "Why do you presume that [your prayer should be heard]? Is it because of the verse 'Let the sinners be consumed' [Psalm 104:35]? But in fact, not 'sinners' is written but 'sins.' Moreover, look at the end of the verse: 'And let the wicked be no more,' which implies that once sins cease, the wicked will be no more. Rather, pray for mercy for them, that they may turn in penitence, so they will be wicked no more." He besought mercy for them, and they turned in penitence.[6]

Again, one of the greatest of the early rabbis is taught a lesson in ethics and scripture by a wife loving enough to rebuke him! Like Beruriah, those spouses courageous and gentle enough to chastise their partners are mentors, generously risking momentary anger or frustration for the sake of inspiring growth of character and soul.

Such devotion permits behavior that would be risky in others. This caring love is not just a matter of ancient history; it happens all the time as spouses summon the courage and faith to chastise their partners in order to help them be better than they otherwise would be.

I recall an older couple in my congregation who were deeply divided over their son's marriage to a non-Jew. The mother, a devout shul-goer, struggled hard to overcome her disappointment and anger at her son's marrying out of the faith. The father, a loyal Jew but less conventionally religious, had an easier time putting his relationship with his son first. The issue that divided them was that on the High Holy Days the son was willing to join his parents for services and for dinner afterward, but the daughter-in-law was willing to join only the family meal. The mother considered this an affront and had told her son and daughter-in-law that if they didn't have the "decency" to sit with her during services, they shouldn't come at all. The dispute had doubly ruptured the family, dividing the parents from their son (and daughter-in-law) and the parents from each other.

In my office one day, both parents recounted their version of the story. Then I watched as the father served as a mentor to his wife.

"Honey," he said, "I know that you love your Judaism and that you wanted our son to marry someone Jewish. I wanted that too, but he hasn't, and however much it hurts, we can't change it. Maybe the best we can do is to show them that Judaism is loving and embracing, and maybe that will influence her to consider our faith too."

At Yom Kippur, when her whole family gathered around the table for the meal before services, they observed the custom of asking whether anyone wished to apologize for anything he or she regretted doing. That year, mustering her courage, the mother apologized to her daughter-in-law for creating an artificial test of her love and for giving her a hard time. The daughter-in-law burst into tears, and the two women embraced amid their tears. That hug would never have happened without the husband's devotion to his wife and his willingness to say something she may not have wanted to hear.

Spouses give the gift of soul by reminding their partners to do better, by willingly risking their mate's rage for the sake of his or her spiritual growth. But the role of mentor is not limited to constructive criticism. Credibility as a mentor demands stalwart loyalty during times of tribulation. The book of Genesis portrays the plight of Isaac and Rebecca: "Isaac pleaded with the Lord on behalf of his wife, because she was barren."[7] Rather than treating the problem as Rebecca's alone, Isaac takes it on himself to pray on her behalf. Rabbinic legend expands on that demonstration of loyalty, claiming that Rebecca, too, refused to see the problem as simply Isaac's. According to the Midrash, "This teaches that Isaac prostrated himself in one spot and she in another. He prayed to God, 'Sovereign of the Universe! May all the children you will grant me be from this righteous woman.' She too prayed likewise."[8] Even in their sorrow, their loyalty to each other remained paramount.

Spouses offer that essential solidarity to each other as the ultimate demonstration of love and commitment. Mentors would do well to emulate that devotion to their *talmidim*.

A therapist at a Jewish Family Service clinic recounted a painful counseling session involving an infertile couple. After the couple had spent a year fruitlessly attempting to conceive and had sought medical intervention, doctors informed them that the man was biologically incapable of creating a child. Devastated, they drove straight to the clinic. Husband, wife, and therapist sat together as the couple talked and sobbed, expressing their distress at having been robbed of their plan to share their love for each other by fashioning a child of their own. Little that the therapist said could soften the blow, so she wisely said little. The climax of their meeting occurred after the man had buried his head in his hands. His wife lifted his hands from his face, cupping them in her own, and she said, "I still love you, and I still want to live my life with you. You are more important to me than even ten children could possibly be."[9]

That breathtaking bond is the soil that allows the soul to bloom. Small wonder, then, that marriage and partnership are the highest expressions of Jewish ideals. Living one's life in the presence of another, learning to consider another's needs as part of one's own, fashioning a future that is shared by two—those are the richest sources of blessing and growth in adult life. To be able to trust another adult sufficiently to allow him or her to critique our deeds and our words and to grow by internalizing the other's perspective and balance—those are the fertile rewards that such a commitment promises. Linking love for a person to a desire to please him or her is the foundation of being an effective mentor. Because spouses want to make each other happy, they are willing to accept the hard work of hearing the other's criticisms and modifying their behavior accordingly. Like a good parent, a loving spouse cannot rely on coercion but must model the kind of productive exchange of views that inspires consent rather than mere conformity.

Teachers

Teachers prepare their students to venture to places and to live fully during times that they themselves will never see. Because of the devotion and time a teacher lavishes on his or her students, a teacher's impact can last a lifetime, extending far beyond the limits of the classroom or the subject matter taught there. Jewish culture acknowledges this centrality of a teacher in a student's life, and the importance of the teacher as mentor appears throughout classical Jewish liturgy. Small wonder, then, that the Midrash records God's insistence that "the teachers of the youth, who perform their work in sincerity and with joy, shall sit at my right hand."[10]

Teachers impart far more than expertise in a particular subject. They help their students cope, and they soften life's rough edges. Perhaps that is why the Talmud observes, "A student's attending upon a sage of Torah is more valuable than even the sage's teaching."[11] Like all mentors, teachers use their personality as a tool, offering the gifts of time and presence. Those gifts provide a context for (and frequently outlast) the content of the class. Students often remember their teacher's wisdom, warmth, or caring long after the intricacies of long division, the stanzas of "The Charge of the Light Brigade," or the details of the Krebs cycle have faded in their memory.

If willing to connect with their students in ways that transcend the classroom, teachers can impart lessons about life itself. A great mentor-as-teacher story involves Hillel when he was an impoverished youth:

> It was reported about Hillel the Elder that every day he used to work and earn one coin, half of which he would give to the guard at the house of learning, the other half being spent for his food and for that of his family. One day he found nothing to earn, and the guard at the house of learning would not permit him to enter. He climbed up and sat upon the window, to hear the words of the living God from the mouth of Sh'mayah and Avtalyon. They say that day was the eve of Sabbath in the winter solstice, and snow fell down upon him from heaven. When the dawn rose, Sh'mayah said to Avtalyon, "Brother

Avtalyon, on every day this house is light and today it is dark. Is it perhaps a cloudy day? They looked up and saw the figure of a man in the window. They went up and found him covered by three cubits of snow. They removed him, bathed and anointed him, and placed him opposite the fire, and they said, "This man deserves that the Sabbath be profaned on his behalf."[12]

This wonderful story involves the most prominent sages of their generation, Sh'mayah and Avtalyon, teaching through kind deeds and learning through the care they extend to the eager Hillel. While the school's official entrance policy prevented poor students from learning, the sages are taught by Hillel's determination that the ability to pay should not be the sole criterion determining who may study in their program. Their openness to learn from Hillel's situation goes quite far: they are willing to violate the laws of the Sabbath (one of the Ten Commandments!) for the sake of including this eager new pupil. Notice that the learning here begins when the gift of presence and the gift of time fuse in a single gesture of welcome and concern.

Such stories of great teaching fill rabbinic literature, testifying to the impact a great teacher can have as mentor. Of Hillel, it is taught that

Once when he concluded his studies with his disciples, Hillel walked along with them. His disciples asked him: "Master, whither are you bound?" He answered them: "To perform a mitzvah." "What," they asked, "is this mitzvah?" He said to them: "To wash in the bathhouse." Said they: "Is this a mitzvah?" "Yes," he replied, "if the statues of kings, which are erected in theaters and circuses, are scoured and washed by the janitor who is appointed to look after them and who thereby obtains a salary through them . . . how much more I, who have been created in the image and likeness of God?" Another time, when Hillel had concluded his studies with his disciples, he walked along with them. His disciples said to him: "Master, where are you going?" He replied: "To bestow kindness upon a guest in the house." They asked: "Have you a guest every day?" He replied: "Is not the poor soul a guest in the body? Today it is here and tomorrow it is here no longer?"[13]

Like any great teacher, Hillel recognized that teaching continues after a lesson has ended. By walking (and living) with his students, he allowed them to question his behavior and learn from his life. To make the teaching come alive requires a teacher who is alive. As the rabbis teach, the words of Torah are compared to fire "to teach you that just as fire does not ignite by itself, so words of Torah do not abide in one who studies alone."[14] A powerful mentor is someone who enflames a student's intellectual curiosity.

Employers and Employees, Colleagues and Community

For most of us, one of life's ironies is that we see the people we care about most only during our "off" hours. Family time is before and after work, with some extra hours thrown in on the weekends. Gathering with friends is limited and may compete with family for the same spare hours. For the bulk of our day, the people we encounter are those with whom we work: employers, employees, colleagues, co-workers. Eight hours a day, five days each week, those people sit near us, work near us, assist or hinder our financial well-being, and further or stymie our career. They may shape our moods, our fortunes, our future.

Because of the proximity, those associates exert a powerful influence on us, and we on them.[15] Learning to mentor at work and learning to let our colleagues guide us are crucial components of spiritual growth and contentment. We learn and teach how to navigate the demands of our profession and how to derive satisfaction from our work. Rather than giving up on our work hours as obligatory and spiritually unengaging, perhaps we can use that time as an opportunity for making insights and improvements.

Our colleagues are often an untapped resource for insights into our profession and enhancement of our responses to the challenges that work and life inevitably present. Rabbinic legend is filled with marvelous examples of rabbis who rely on the wisdom of their colleagues to augment their own:

Rabbi Hiyya bar Abba fell ill and Rabbi Yohanan went in to visit him. He said to him: "Are your sufferings welcome to you?" He replied: "Neither they nor their reward." He said to him: "Give me your hand." He gave him his hand and he raised him.

Rabbi Yohanan once fell ill and Rabbi Hanina went in to visit him. He said to him: "Are your sufferings welcome to you?" He replied: "Neither they nor their reward." He said to him: "Give me your hand." He gave him his hand and he raised him. Why could not Rabbi Yohanan raise himself? They replied: the prisoner cannot free himself from jail.

Rabbi Eliezer fell ill and Rabbi Yohanan went in to visit him. He noticed that he was lying in a dark room, and Rabbi Yohanan bared his arm and light radiated from it. Thereupon he noticed that Rabbi Eliezer was weeping, and he said to him: "Why do you weep? Is it because you did not study enough Torah? Surely we learned [in Tractate Menahot]: 'The one who sacrifices much and the one who sacrifices little have the same merit, provided that the heart is directed to heaven.'[16] Is it perhaps lack of sustenance? Not everybody has the privilege to enjoy two tables. Is it perhaps because of [the lack of] children? This is the bone of my tenth son!" He replied to him: "I am weeping on account of this beauty that is going to rot in the earth." He said to him: "On that account you surely have a reason to weep"; and they both wept. In the meanwhile he said to him: "Are your sufferings welcome to you?" He replied: "Neither they nor their reward." He said to him: "Give me your hand," and he gave him his hand and he raised him.[17]

These stories offer a poignant truth: we can be mentors to each other and offer support for the challenges in each other's lives. However, we become helpless and baffled by the afflictions of our experience. No matter how wise or insightful we may be, to be good mentors we must know how and when to rely on other mentors. Whereas Rabbi Yohanan was fully capable of healing his colleague, he, too, needed the help of a colleague when he himself fell ill. When he thought he was performing the mitzvah of *bikur holim* (visiting the sick) to mentor his friend and associate Rabbi Eliezer, it turned out that it was Rabbi Eliezer who taught Rabbi Yohanan something about mortality, life, and what really counts. At the same time that Rabbi Eliezer was a mentor to Yohanan, he relied on Rabbi Yohanan to heal him. The relationship of mentor to *talmid* doesn't flow in just one direction, nor does it preclude the possibility of being a mentor to one's mentor or learning from one's disciples. As we teach, we learn; as we learn, we teach—often from the very same individual.

That ancient process of growing through the care of others continues to this day, as the following story illustrates. I met Susan at a Young Leadership retreat. When Susan moved to a new community, she knew no one there. Wandering into a deli one day, she fell into a conversation with another woman, JoAnne, and they ate their lunches together. Before her meal was over, Susan's new acquaintance had invited her to attend a program hosted by the women's division of the local Federation chapter. At that meeting, Susan signed up to work on an upcoming luncheon and so began to spend more time with JoAnne. JoAnne continued to offer advice, helped Susan make connections to other women, and even flew with Susan to her first meeting of the General Assembly. Today Susan is chair of that same women's division and a recognized leader in her community. When you ask her how all that happened, she answers with one word, "JoAnne."

In our work, volunteer positions, and community associations, we establish mutually educational relationships, a kind of relationship that is not new to Jewish society. The sages of antiquity, too, were often in a position to learn difficult lessons from the members of their community, as this story shows:

> Once the house of the patriarch ordained a fast and no rain fell. Thereupon Oshaiah, a young rabbi [gave a sermon highly critical of the patriarch, who was deeply offended by the young rabbi's impudence]. . . Thereupon the soldiers of the patriarch came and put a scarf around his neck and tortured him. Whereupon the people of the city cried out, "Leave him alone! He also insults us, but since we see that whatever he does is for the sake of heaven, we say nothing to him and we leave him alone, so you too leave him alone."[18]

Jewish institutional life hasn't changed so much, has it? It's easy to picture Oshaiah, fresh from his professional training, filled with book learning and the eagerness (and arrogance) that only the young and untested can exhibit. Zealous in his calling, he gets high marks for passion and conviction but doesn't score so well on compassion or diplomacy. When he gives a sermon that criticizes the leading Jewish authority of his age, the patriarch responds by sending out his soldiers to beat some sense and deference into this brand-new rabbi. The townspeople, experienced in such things, know that a young rabbi often needs some time to realize that the simple solutions of his books and his teachers don't always work in the real world.

Apparently what is true today was true then, too: wise rabbis mellow with time. Age and experience form the gateway to moderation and to wisdom. So the townsfolk rallied to protect their rabbi for they knew that his heart was in the right place. I imagine that his impression of his community was profoundly shaped by that day and that he must have mulled over the lessons of his congregants' intervention for quite a long time.

Each of us is called into the service of something larger than ourselves. Life is a gift, unanticipated and unearned. Blessed with such a boon, we can choose to cherish life fully by sharing the lessons we learn along the way. We can nurture each other's soul and receive nourishment from each other at the same time. In our communities, in associates at work, in colleagues, and in spouses, we have rich resources for guidance, support, and connection. And we can nurture each other's soul. Our spiritual journey can find sustenance in the experiences and teachings of our fellow travelers through life.

Becoming Better Leaders
and Mentors

Chapter Five

Can Anyone Be a Mentor?

> *Books are not now the prime need of the day. But what*
> *we need more than ever, or at least as much as ever, are*
> *human beings.*
>
> —Franz Rosenzweig, "On Education"

Yes, you can be a mentor. In fact, not only can you be a mentor, but odds are you already *are* a mentor to a good many people who are part of the personal, professional, and communal aspects of your life.

None of us is perfect. Most of us must struggle to integrate our life experiences into the tasks of refining our character and our commitments. Yet it is precisely our shared wrestling with temptation and imperfection that links us to each other, qualifying us to be mentors, to pass along the rich and beautiful life that is Judaism. That ageless transmission requires conscious effort, however. It materializes neither through abstract philosophy (although philosophy and theology provide important tools along the way) nor through behavioral ideals (although such aspirations are vitally important). What translates thinking and idealized deed into life is a fellow human being willing to serve as a guide and a companion. As Martin Buber reminded us,

> The teachings themselves are the way. Their full content is not comprehended in any book, in any code, in any formulation. Nothing that has ever existed is broad enough to show what they are. In order

that they may live and bring forth life, generations must continue to meet, and the teachings assume the form of a human link, awakening and activating our common bond with our Father. The spark that leaps from him who teaches to him who learns rekindles a spark of that fire which lifted the mountain of revelation "to the very heart of heaven."[1]

Working with the malleable stuff of humanity, we can offer others a ladder of perfectibility through a life of Jewish learning and observance. Character is not engraved in stone. In the words of the Rambam, "From one's youth, one becomes accustomed to acting in accordance with the accepted behavior of family and locale."[2] If our immediate family is *am Yisrael,* the Jewish people (and our extended family is all humanity), and our neighborhood is the Torah (while our hometown is the cosmos itself), then we can hope to accustom ourselves to very high standards indeed. One of the truths of human life is that we need each other to know ourselves truly.

Our capacity to ignore our flaws, to evade our calling, is both persistent and deep. It takes a loving companion and a courageous colleague, a mentor, to draw our attention to our foibles. A willingness to step forward and be such a mentor is a precious gift.

The recognition that we have the power to mold each other's character and that we need each other expresses one of Judaism's fundamentally positive affirmations of human potential: that we can become better than we are. We each have the potential to improve. Humans are not born evil, nor are they tainted by sinfulness as a pervasive condition. Instead, Judaism holds each of us responsible for our deeds (and our community) precisely because it believes in our ability to be the captains of our soul.

Far from reflecting a simple naïveté, Jewish tradition recognizes that people have the capacity for good *and* evil, that we oscillate between our *yetzer hatov,* a good inclination, and our *yetzer hara,* an evil inclination. The goodness within is only potential; it requires diligent effort to become dominant. As Rabbi Hayyim Luzzatto explains,

"Although saintliness is latent in the character of every normal person . . . [it is] not so innate as to enable people to dispense with the effort needed to develop it."[3] This process of character formation is sometimes seen as solitary, inner work. Yet Judaism joins with other voices in insisting that the self is social at its core, that the notion of an autonomous self separable from the community is an impossibility and a lie.[4] From the moment of birth, consciousness coalesces in the context of relationship—with mother, father, siblings, community, world. We are who we are in relation to others. Viewed in this more holistic way, the self is never isolated; it is an expression of the blend of static and dynamic. One's self emerges from the dance of individual characteristics molding and being molded by those parts of the world we connect with: our family, culture, religion, experiences, and relationships. The nature of selfhood means we are always capable of change, always ready for growth. But human growth, like gardening, requires care—preparing the soil, watering, pruning, tending. Soul growth requires constant attention.

Because it is necessary to train in order to be good and sensitive, people need to see living examples of others who are one or two steps farther down the spiritual road. Moral development is incremental— seeing someone who is just a little more advanced makes it possible to identify and progress toward one's goal. Mentors offer that living example. Helping to locate areas that need work and sharing their own inner journey are the invaluable tools that a mentor can provide.

Mentors Are Flawed

Many of us are ambivalent about the idea of mentoring precisely because we expect holy men or holy women to be without fault, to know all the answers, and to embody perfection. How reassuring, then, to see the mentor of mentors, Moshe Rabbenu, openly confronting God and doubting God's justice. He did this precisely because of his love for his people. In other words, it is *because* he learned from his temper and his imperfect faith that Moses was able to be a mentor. Moses did not have all the answers,[5] but he was willing to pose questions. Like us, he struggled with theological uncertainties, and he railed against the injustices that too often abounded. What made Moses a mentor was his refusal to abandon his God or his people because of that struggle. And what was true for Moses is no less true for us: it is in the giving that we grow and in the act of caring that our hearts expand in godliness. It is not the goal that is foremost, but the way.

In addressing itself to the service of the *kohanim* (the biblical priests in the Tabernacle), the Torah states, "No one of your offspring throughout the ages who has a *mum* [defect] shall be qualified to offer food to God; no one who has a *mum* shall be qualified."[6]

Schooled in the historical method, a biblical scholar's first defense against a troubling verse in the Torah is to quarantine it securely in its historical context, so let's begin our contemplation of this verse by using that approach. The *kohen* in the Temple was to be a symbol of perfection; because the rituals the priest performed were physical, his perfection had to be physical. This perfection was understood by the biblical mind as *sh'leimut* (wholeness). The *kohen* couldn't be missing any part, therefore, because he had to symbolize wholeness in the presence of God. Indeed, as the Torah goes on to state, "One who has a *mum* shall not enter behind the *parochet* [curtain separating the Torah in the Holy Ark], nor come near the altar."[7]

But history cannot remove our discomfort with this precept. Are we saying that a person can't draw near God or serve on behalf of the community if he or she has a *mum*? Is there anyone among us who is perfect? Is there anyone here—or anywhere—who doesn't in fact manifest not only one *mum* but many? Is it possible that only those who are perfect are capable of serving God and each other? Certainly on a literal level, this has not been true in Jewish life. Our father Jacob limps his way into greatness. Moses speaks what are surely history's greatest speeches with a speech impediment. The Talmud, too, relates the lives of great figures—Nahum ish Gamzo, Rav Sheshet, and others—who with, and perhaps because of, their physical challenges (in these instances, quadriplegia and blindness), attained spiritual greatness. It is theologically certain that the only one who is perfect is God. Can it be, then, that only God can serve?

The Torah poses and then responds to this very question: "Is corruption then God's? No, God's children are the ones who are blemished."[8] A rabbinic genius turns the verse on its head: "Even though they are full of blemishes, they are still God's children."[9]

We are God's children—blemishes, defects, imperfections, and all—and we cannot afford to allow our shortcomings to prevent us from offering bold leadership, from taking the responsibility to do good or glorify Torah as we might. So let's try a different percolation of that crucial verse in Leviticus. Let's consider the fact that the one thing a person cannot ever truly have is a defect. A defect is a lack of something. How can we possess that which we lack? What we have when we have a *mum* is not a lack of something but rather the *perception* of lacking something. A *mum* is possible only if we construe ourselves as somehow deficient.

A *mum*, then, is a shortfall that makes us feel incomplete. It is the part of some imaginary whole that can exist only in the mind. I would like to propose, then, that *sh'leimut* (wholeness) does not mean physical perfection. Indeed, it is not perfection of any kind. *Sh'leimut* means serving God with all our being, with the entirety of who we are, without leaving any part of ourselves outside the divine service: "with all your heart, with all your soul, with all your might."[10] God doesn't demand of us that we apportion ourselves into little pieces, some parts of which are kosher, some parts of which are acceptable, some parts of which may be public, and the rest of which must be hidden away. It is that hiding that is the *mum*, and a person with a *mum* can neither serve the Holy One nor stand before an imperfect community pretending to be perfect.

We can serve the Eternal only with the wholeness that comes from imperfection, with our entire being, with both positive and negative traits—as Rashi (Rabbi Shlomo Yitzhak, the great French Bible and Talmud commentator) said, "with both your inclinations." We can serve the Holy One only if our entire existence is brought with us into the divine service. Perhaps, then, the wholeness to which the Torah alludes is a willingness to stand in our entirety—blemishes, defects, imperfections, and all—and offer our complete self to God as a sacred service. Might the Torah be insisting on a community that includes *all* its members, that makes none of them invisible, that asks none of them to step outside? Might only that community be a community fit to offer sacrifices that God will accept?

As mentors, let us bring our entire being to the service of God and humanity. Let us keep no part of ourselves outside. Let us leave no piece invisible. The Talmud reminds us, "God wants the heart."[11] We can teach the Jews with whom we will serve that they, too, are precious and that all of them, because of their imperfections, are truly God's children. We can teach them not to postpone encountering Torah, living mitzvot, building community, or assuring a vibrant future until the day when they are perfect—such a day will never come! We must remind them that the Torah was not given to angels. We are all blemished; human wholeness comes not from some elusive perfection but rather from the radical act of taking hold of our imperfections and offering even them in our relationships. It is recorded that Hillel had the audacity to speak on God's behalf. Taking my cue from him, I muster the audacity to extend Hillel's insight beyond God's presence to our own, as ours is a reflection of the Divine Presence. God (if not Hillel) would want it that way. *"Im ani kan, hakol kan"* ("If I am here," says God, "all is here").[12] Who knows but that for God to be truly present, our all must also be truly present. In the words of the twentieth-century poet Aaron Zeitlin:

Praise Me, says God, I will know that you love Me.
Curse Me, I will know that you love Me.
Praise Me or curse Me,
I will know that you love Me.
Sing out My graces, says God.
Raise your fist against Me and revile, says God.
Sing My graces or revile,
Reviling is also praise, says God.
But if you sit fenced off in apathy,
Entrenched in "I don't give a damn," says God,
If you look at the stars and yawn, says God,
If you see suffering and don't cry out,
If you don't praise and don't revile,
Then I created you in vain, says God.

In all moments, we can celebrate that presence and inspire the Jews whose lives we touch to feel it. As it was for our limping ancestor Jacob, what matters is not that we overcome our struggles but that we don't accept them passively.

Chapter Six

The Virtues of a Mentor

This is what the Holy One said to Israel,
"My children, I have withheld nothing from you.
What do I seek from you?
I seek no more than that you love one another
And honor one another."

—TANNA DE–VEI ELIYAHU

The affirmation that we are made in God's image makes it possible for anyone to be a mentor and for us to be mentors to others. To become capable of teaching and nurturing others while achieving one's own spiritual depth requires attention, patience, and preparation. Those virtues don't erupt full blown in a single instant. Instead, they are the rich harvest of a life's steady work. Let's explore the core virtues we must cultivate in order to become mentors to other seeking souls, and let's consider precisely how a mentor-to-be goes about acquiring such worthy attributes.

Virtues of Integrity

The first virtue a mentor requires is integrity. As one Talmudic rabbi claimed, "My mouth reflects my heart."[1] Integrity—the correspondence between how we present ourselves and who we truly are—is the fundamental basis for serving as a role model. Clearly a mentor cannot be a helpful guide if the one who is served cannot count on the mentor's honesty and trustworthiness. Thus Rabbi Shimon bar Yoḥai understood God to say to Israel, "If you retain your water-clear integrity, then I shall be the Holy One your God."[2]

As laudable as integrity may be, it poses a challenge from the start. If we must reveal our true nature, then all our flaws, faults, and idiosyncrasies become public property. We have already seen that we can indeed be mentors and yet not embody all of the Torah's notions of the ideal Jew. While some mentors of the past may have been seen as flawless and ethereal, such a posture is impossible for us in today's world. In present times, the people we encounter would rightly distrust such perfection, considering it artifice. Integrity doesn't require perfection; it requires only reliability and responsibility for one's actions.

Fortunately, for most of us even the most influential guide is blemished. Imperfect people cannot benefit from role models they can never hope to emulate. Judaism presents a radical model of greatness, one measured by flaws overcome, lessons learned, and temptations resisted. I will never forget an incident I witnessed while still a rabbinical student. The rabbi's error, and subsequent apology, remain with me to this day as a powerful example of helping others to learn from one's own flaws. While visiting a synagogue, I watched a great rabbi teach a powerful lesson precisely because of a momentary lapse in judgment. With the best of intentions (although perhaps not the best of discretion), the rabbi called up a young girl during the Torah service and formally "named" her Cabbage Patch doll. As he offered this unusual prayer, I saw the president and vice president of the synagogue stand and storm out of the sanctuary, visibly angered. After the Torah was returned to the Ark, the rabbi was summoned from the room. When he returned, accompanied by the synagogue officers, he looked chastened and sad. He ascended the podium once again and confessed, "I owe the congregation an apology. I blessed a Cabbage Patch doll today because I wanted to find a way to include the children in the service. But what I did might appear to belittle the wonder of naming a baby and may well have caused offense. I've learned from this mistake and want to thank the president for pointing it out to me." Then he sat down. What a dazzling model of a mentor, willing to learn from his mistakes and willing to share them with his flock! Such a flawed mentor is a truly great role model.

Consider the personalities in the book of Genesis: none of the patriarchs or matriarchs is irreproachable. The families of the first book of the Torah indulge in sibling rivalry, spousal jealousy, disastrous sexism, drug abuse, sexual immorality, theft, violence, and murder, and as parents they can appear to be distant or impartial.[3] That same realism spills over into the rest of the Torah: the family of Moses is troubled by jealousy and competition, tragedy and bloodshed, though also blessed with great loyalty and joy. These men and women are remarkable not because of their perfection but because of how they responded to their deficiencies. They are compelling role models today because they mustered sufficient spiritual strength to meet the challenges that life (and their relatives) cast their way. In the process, they offer hope and possibility to us, their distant—and still blemished—descendants.

What is stirring about the towering figures of the Bible is not just that they exemplify a marred (hence useful) integrity but that each mentor is unique and true to his or her distinctive character. Isaac does not try to mimic Abraham, and Rachel is different from Rebecca. Each achieved greatness while being true to himself or herself. A Ḥasidic tale underscores the value of this integrity:

> After Rabbi Noah's succession as rabbi at Lechivitz, some Ḥasidim inquired of him, "Why don't you conduct yourself like your father, the late rabbi?" "I do conduct myself like him," retorted Rabbi Noah. "He did not imitate anybody, and I likewise do not imitate anybody."[4]

Still, integrity is more than merely being true to oneself and one's individuality. Integrity also means being true to higher values regarding what is right and good. Rabbi Abraham Joshua Heschel was such a mentor, one who was able to live the values he preached and studied. Through a lifetime of studying the prophets of Israel, he came to realize that Judaism demands involvement in social justice as a form of the service to God. He marched next to Dr. Martin Luther King Jr. in Selma, Alabama, and afterward proclaimed, "My feet were praying!" Risking his academic credentials for the sake of righteousness, Rabbi Heschel made his commitment to the civil rights movement a central expression of his piety. He protested U.S. involvement in Vietnam on religious grounds, as a result receiving a visit from two representatives of the State Department. The agents told him that his public opposition to the Vietnam War might induce President Lyndon Johnson to weaken his commitment to Israel. In a remarkable moment of integrity and courage, Rabbi Heschel expelled the bureaucrats from his office. The rabbi understood that a spiritual mentor has to live by the Torah's command to "do what is right and good in the sight of the Eternal One."[5]

A life lived according to Torah presents an opportunity to grow in sensitivity and holiness. But it promises no more than a potential and a path. Whereas many have used the Torah's commandments to refine their spiritual lives, others have attended to the Torah's details while evading its elevated imperatives. In a stunning display of self-awareness and honesty, the sages conceded that the study and practice of Torah do not necessarily equal goodness: "Rava contrasted [two biblical verses]: It is written 'My teaching shall fall like the rain,' and it is written, 'My speech shall flow like the dew' [Deuteronomy 32:2]. If a Torah scholar is of good character, it is like dew; and if not, it breaks his neck like a rainstorm."[6]

One can be a great scholar and still be immoral. Torah offers the possibility of self-restraint and moral elevation, but far too many can obsess on its details while sidestepping its goals. The Talmud repeatedly describes the gap between the ideal Torah scholar and the Torah scholar who seems to have missed the point of all that study:

But if someone studies scripture and Mishnah attends to the disciples of the wise but is dishonest in business and rude to other people, they say, "Woe to the one who studies Torah, to the parents and the teacher who taught this one Torah. This one studied Torah and, look, such corrupt deeds and ugly ways." Of such a person, scripture says, "These are the people of the Holy One and are gone forth out of God's land."[7]

To be someone's mentor, it is crucial to couple one's knowledge and love of Torah with moral decency and compassion. One of today's towering giants of integrity is Rabbi Elliot Dorff, provost of the University of Judaism in Los Angeles and one of the leading theologians and *poskim* (decisors, scholars who rule on matter of *halachah*) of Conservative Judaism. Those who have studied with Rabbi Dorff revere him because he respects his students and because his integrity is beyond question. Over a long and shining career, no one has ever so much as questioned his honesty, his character, or his goodness. Hence, when he offers an opinion, his listeners know that he himself would follow the advice. He insists on the importance of *g'milut hasadim* (deeds of loving-kindness) and is an active leader of the Jewish Family Service. He preaches the importance of involving children in community and in programing, and he has taught at Camp Ramah during countless summers. He sets a standard for *tzedakah* that few can equal. Time and again, his life measures up to his preaching, making it possible for those who encounter him to take his proclamations seriously. In recent debates on the role of both gay men and women in the context of Jewish law, Rabbi Dorff has been an outspoken advocate on behalf of their inclusion and equality. That stance might have marginalized someone with a less solid character, yet because of his unimpeachable integrity, even ideological opponents stop and listen.

So important is the role of integrity that Jewish law insists, "People should not go to study with a teacher who does not walk in the good way—even though that teacher might be a great sage and might be needed by the people. They must not study with that person until the teacher reforms."[8] The integrity and honesty of the mentor are no less requirements for his or her character than are a love of learning and a respect for observance.

Virtues of Caring and Empathy

When my rebbe, Rabbi Simon Greenberg of blessed memory, was honored on the occasion of his ninetieth birthday, he was praised for his great learning and his active leadership. But no less inspiring were the stories of how much he loved people and extended himself for them. Once while eating lunch in a restaurant, he conversed with the waiter, a young man who revealed that he was a new immigrant without the funds to attend college. After reflecting for only a moment, Rabbi Greenberg offered to pay for his entire education, and for the next several years he did precisely that. But he offered far more than just money. Rabbi Greenberg regularly met with the young man to discuss his studies and life. Offering himself as a mentor and a guide, Rabbi Greenberg literally—financially and spiritually—gave the young man a future. Such is the power of a mentor's love for his disciple.

In addition to showing Rabbi Greenberg to be a person of integrity, that story displays the importance of a mentor being approachable, encouraging, and genuinely interested in the protégé's concerns. According to Rabbi Ḥanina bar Papa, "When you teach a child scripture, teach in a spirit of awe; an equanimous face for Mishnah; a friendly face for Talmud; a joyous face for *aggadah*."[9] For Rabbi Ḥanina, the imprimatur for teaching with joy and friendliness comes from none other than God, since "the Holy One appeared to Israel with an awe-inspiring face, with an equanimous face, a friendly face, a joyous face."[10] That God appears to the people of Israel with a visage of acceptance and love is a decisive influence for mentoring and teaching. Teaching Torah must be done in a context of acceptance: the mode of teaching must itself embody the values taught.

Janet Harris is an educator who has directed the family program at Camp Ramah in California for many years. Each summer as the families arrive at the camp, Janet greets each parent and child by name, a task that requires hours of preparation and concentrated study for those brief moments of interaction. Before commencing any formal Jewish teaching, she sets the tone and context for the Jewish learning that will take place that summer. Her welcome is an integral component of her Torah. Her actions echo the manners of the great sages of antiquity: "It is said of Rabban Yoḥanan ben Zakai that no one ever greeted him first, not even a heathen in the marketplace."[11] Making sure to welcome others by so simple an act as greeting them first is an essential component of what being a mentor is all about.

A mentor who is arrogant or haughty will find it almost impossible to be truly accessible or empathetic. The concerns of another just won't seem sufficiently important to merit the mentor's notice. I learned that lesson from one of the most powerful men I've ever had the privilege to meet. When I was eighteen, I volunteered as an intern to Alan Cranston. He was then the majority whip, the third most powerful person in the U.S. Senate. I had just completed my freshman year of college and worked in his district office in San Francisco. One day I was instructed to drive to the airport, pick up the senator, and drive him back to the office. I was both thrilled and terrified to have the chance to meet such a prominent man face-to-face, or at least through a rear-view mirror. On the ride to the office, Senator Cranston asked my name and proceeded to inquire about my schooling, ambitions, and life. I was impressed by his political skills—he made it look as if he took me seriously—but I assumed he was just being gracious and passing the time. A month later, I chauffeured the senator again. This time he got into my car and without prompting said, "Hello, Brad." Then he proceeded to ask follow-up questions based on our conversation of the month before. He cared enough to remember the particulars of my life! By his example, Senator Cranston taught me that true greatness lies in valuing every person you encounter, no matter what his or her station is in life in comparison with your own.

If we hope to be approachable and embracing, we must respect those we teach or supervise. Mutual respect may sound like an easy assignment; however, it is far too tempting to dismiss the opinions we disagree with by attacking the intelligence or morals of our opponents. Even in the realm of religion, we often divide into hostile camps, deafening ourselves to the perspectives of those with whom we disagree. The traditionalists are "sexist," "homophobic," or "fossilized"; the progressives are "relativistic," "weak," or "faddish." Such derisive labeling makes our hearing each other impossible. Beyond issues of content or conflicting loyalties, it is often difficult to muster respect for those who seem less intelligent or less knowledgeable and stubbornly maintain an opinion that differs from ours. To be mentors, we need to respect the people we argue with, the people whose lives we hope to touch.

Moses and Aaron were towering leaders of the Jewish people, and they were brothers. The Torah records their closeness and it records more challenging moments (like Aaron's permitting the building of the Golden Calf). Yet the rabbis choose to highlight the brothers' efforts to maintain their mutual respect; their high regard for each other is precisely what allows the emergence of God's voice: "Rabbi Shimon bar Yoḥai said, 'Moses would show respect to Aaron by saying, "Teach me," and Aaron would show similar respect to Moses by saying, "Teach me."' As a result, God's words came from between them, and it was as if both were speaking."[12]

In a similar tale of intellectual dispute between players of mutual regard, the Midrash praises two great mentors: "Whenever Rabbi Yoshiah and Rabbi Matiah ben Heresh would study Torah together, they argued heatedly. And when they parted, they treated each other like childhood friends."[13] This remarkable combination—a no-holds-barred approach to argumentation for the sake of Torah combined with collegial affection despite strong religious differences—is one of the defining traits of rabbinic Judaism and one of its greatest contributions to harmony and rational discourse. The rabbis insisted on maintaining a sense of their friendship despite their disputes and thus were able to spur each other on to a deeper understanding of what the Torah might mean. A corollary expression of mutual regard is a willingness to learn from anybody, no matter what that person's outlook on life or social status. As one ancient source insisted,

> The Holy Blessing One said, "If a person of modest scholarly attainments tells you something and you derive spiritual delight from the insight, do not regard it as something you heard from an inferior scholar. Moreover, you must even regard it as having been told you by a great sage. . . . And even more than that! You must regard it as if you had heard it from God directly."[14]

If we are able to regard anyone who teaches us anything as God's representative, if anything we learn is an expansion of the Torah of Moses, then anyone can be our mentor and we can see God in every person. One of my favorite moments of unanticipated learning occurred when I was teaching a group of preschool children about Hanukkah. After recounting the story of the Maccabees and their battle for freedom, I asked the three- and four-year-olds what it means to be free. One child called out, "Being free means I get to be with my family." A second volunteered, "Being free is having milk and cookies." And a third child offered, "Being free is when I get to play with my toys." I can't think of a better definition of freedom: having the ability to associate with those we choose, having adequate food and shelter, having the ability to do what we desire. Those children were the mentors that day.[15]

Virtues of Teaching

As we have already discussed, a mentor is not just a guide but also a teacher. Our text is not only the Torah of the Five Books of Moses or even the Torah of rabbinic wisdom; it is also the Torah (teaching) of all of God's Creation. Such teaching can be lasting only if conducted with patience, only if the disciple enjoys access to the mentor, and only if there is sufficient involvement on the part of the mentor.

What are some of the characteristics of an ideal teacher? The first skill a teacher must cultivate is an openness to each student's style, personality, and pace. In short, a mentor must be patient. Patience is such an important trait that the rabbis understood it to be a biblical imperative: "A person must train to be calm, as it says, 'Remove anger from your heart' [Kohelet 11:10]."[16]

A tale is told of the great sage Hillel, whose patience was legendary. With that trait of his in mind, two men took bets on whether one of them would be able to make Hillel lose his temper. One kept interrupting the sage, during a bath and during his sleep, each time asking seemingly trivial questions of Jewish law or practice. Each time, the sage responded seriously to the question, willing to give a careful and engaged response. Finally the man realized that he could not make Hillel angry and could not provoke the mentor, causing him to stop answering the questions. In frustration and amazement, he blurted out: "On your account, I have lost four hundred *zuz*." Hillel said, "Calm your spirit. Losing four hundred *zuz*, and even an additional four hundred *zuz*, was well worth it, [for you have learned that whatever the provocation] Hillel will not lose his temper."[17]

Hillel understood that the time to answer a question is when it is asked and that an inquiry that seems trivial or bothersome to a teacher may well transform the student who is asking. Beyond the specific content of Hillel's answer is the reassurance that the mentor will devote time, attention, and thought to the priorities and concerns of the *talmid*, the willing, eager student. Hillel's story teaches us that patience is more than just resignation in the face of someone's slower pace or a decision to respond thoroughly to another person's intrusion.

Patience ought to embrace something larger: a willingness to set aside one's agenda in order to focus on the needs or desires of another person. The Talmud teaches, "Someone impatient is unfit to be a rebbe."[18] People learn at different rates and often according to different plans. There is no single path to wholeness or holiness. Each student possesses a unique configuration of skills, abilities, and manners of receptivity. Consequently, there is no single approach that will work for every student in the same way or at the same time.

Dr. Temple Grandin, a prominent professor of animal sciences, offers an example of such a mentor in her book *Thinking in Pictures*.[19] As a baby, Grandin was diagnosed as autistic, and she grew up facing the unique challenges that this disability poses. One of her high-school teachers was particularly sensitive to her needs and gifts. He noticed that unlike most other students, Grandin thought nonverbally—in pictures rather than words. So he guided her toward working with animals because animals also think in pictures. Encouraged by his gentle push and superb intuition, she now has a doctorate in animal sciences and has refashioned the method of animal slaughter in commercial slaughterhouses across the United States so that it takes place in a more humane fashion. Not surprisingly, this commitment to humane slaughter has drawn Grandin to reflect on the laws of kashrut, which also emphasize the most humane and least painful methods of animal slaughter and cultivate in Jews who follow them a mindfulness to reflect on when the choice is made to take a life in order to provide sustenance. Grandin's writings include abundant reflections on kashrut (the Jewish dietary laws) and the Jewish value of *tza'ar ba'alei hayim* (minimizing the pain of living things). Grandin lives independently, has established a national reputation, and enjoys a prosperous career. Inspired by her teachers, she has made a second career as a public speaker, offering hope to people with autism and their families. Grandin's high-school teacher was a great mentor: not only did he recognize that this student had distinctive gifts to offer, but his example also set the tone for her path as a mentor.

Related to patience is the virtue of accessibility. In the judgment of the ancient rabbis one who is too busy studying to attend to the needs of a widow or orphan is guilty of destroying the world. That same admonition characterizes a key difference between the house of Shammai and its primary competitor in the early rabbinic world, the house of Hillel:

> "And raise many students" [*Avot* 1:1]. Beit Shammai says, "A person should teach only those who are wise, humble, and a descendant of distinguished people, and wealthy." Beit Hillel says, "A person should teach everyone, for there were many Jewish sinners who became attached to Torah study, and as a result, righteous, pious, and decent people came from them."[20]

By providing access to their teachings, the mentors of the house of Hillel were able to enlighten people whom others considered unworthy of the effort. Access to those great teachers made all the difference for the "undesirable" students.

To be someone's mentor requires making oneself accessible to one's *talmidim,* responding to their letters, e-mail messages, and phone calls and to their need to meet in person. We must accept that it takes time to be someone's mentor.

Virtues of the Soul

The capstone to a mentor's art is the gift of soul. Above all else, a mentor seeks to light a spark, to enable a *talmid* to ignite his or her studies with a passion for life, for Judaism, for God, for righteousness and compassion. Integrity and patience can create the context in which such passion is exposed and shared. But success requires an additional condition: mentors must love Torah; they must be lifelong students of the scriptures they teach, and—almost as important—they must be open to the realm of the sacred and the introduction of God into daily life.

A mentor expresses a love of Torah by the amount of time and energy he or she dedicates to its study. Without constant analysis and review, it is impossible to retain an intimacy with the Torah; it is impossible to access its many layers of wisdom. "Turn it and turn it, for all is in it," taught a great ancient mentor,[21] and that advice still holds. Anyone who would transmit Torah must labor at Torah.

While it is true that anything can become Torah if it is studied in order to learn about God or God's Creation, it is also true that the Torah can cease to be Torah if it is approached without reverence and purpose. Rabbi Bernie King once taught, "Before reading the Torah to see what you want to teach, try reading it to see what it can teach you." If a scholar reads the book of Exodus only as a way to uncover ancient Near Eastern thought or to investigate ancient conceptions of divinity as a historical construct, such study precludes experiencing God's will or love. The Baal Shem Tov crafted an exaggerated dichotomy when he insisted that "study for the sake of scholarship is desecration; it is a transgression of the mitzvah against bowing before alien gods, the idol being mere learning. The study of the Torah is a matter of the heart's devotion."[22] Such historical inquiries, valuable though they might be in providing helpful background, are not in themselves Torah. Only when seeking God and pursuing learning does talmud Torah emerge.[23] The Talmud teaches, "A person should not say, 'I will study the written Torah so I will be called sage. I will study the oral Torah so that I will be called rabbi.' . . . Rather, study out of a sense of love and eventually the study will come of its own."[24]

Before we worry about teaching, we need to focus on learning. As a Hasidic mentor reminded a student: "Don't tell me how often you've gone through the Talmud; tell me how many times the Talmud has gone through you." It is time to reestablish the priority of reading the Torah (or the Talmud or any holy text) with an eye toward asking, "What does the Holy One require of me now? What is God saying to me through this passage today?" Only then will we learn something worth teaching.

The Sages Have the Last Word

The same characteristics that define a caring Jewish individual also emanate from the core of a mentor. With a temperament molded by honesty, a pedagogy informed by patience, and a soul elevated by reverence of Torah (and of the One speaking through Torah), a mentor is well equipped to help shape and nurture lives and institutions.

Are these the only characteristics that it takes to be a mentor? Surely not. One can easily imagine that this is the short list and that a longer list would only enhance our ability as mentors. For such a list, let us allow the sages of old to have the last word (and be sure to read the last virtue!):

> Torah is acquired through forty-eight virtues: by study; by attentiveness; by orderly speech; by an understanding heart; by a perceptive heart; by awe; by reverence; by humility; by joy; by ministering to the sages; by cleaving to colleagues; by acute discussion with *talmidim;* by calmness in study; by study of scripture and Mishnah; by a minimum of business; by a minimum of sleep; by a minimum of small talk; by a minimum of worldly pleasure; by a minimum of frivolity; by a minimum of worldly pursuits; by patience; by a generous heart; by trust in the sages; by acceptance of suffering; by knowing one's place; by contentment with one's lot; by guarding one's speech; by taking no personal credit; by being beloved; by loving God; by loving all creatures; by loving charitable deeds; by loving rectitude; by loving reproof; by shunning honor; by not boasting of one's learning; by not delighting in rendering decisions; by sharing the burden with one's fellow; by influencing one's fellow to virtue; by setting one's fellow on the path of truth; by setting one's fellow on the path of peace; by concentrating on one's studies; by asking and answering questions; by absorbing knowledge and contributing to it; by studying in order to teach and to perform mitzvot; by sharpening the wisdom of one's teacher; by being precise in transmitting what one has learned; by quoting one's source.[25]

Chapter Seven

A Mentor's Communication Skills

> *Happy is the generation in which the greater give ear to the lesser.*
>
> —Rosh Hashanah

Listening to Our Voices. . . and Learning to Hear Them

If we wish to act as mentors and nurture others on the path to wholeness and holiness, we must discipline ourselves to listen well. To do so, we must recognize that "some speak with their eyes, some with their hands, some with the shaking of their head, some with the movement of their body, and some with their feet."[1] To show a speaker that he or she is the sole focus of our attention, we must demonstrate the skill of active listening, through eye contact, posture, verbal acknowledgment, and facial expressions. Without active listening, we preclude communication. And without communication, there can be no learning, no growth, and no relationship.

As we have done before, we can look to Moses as an exemplar—this time one of mindfulness and active listening. When God summons Moses to ascend Mount Sinai to receive the Ten Commandments, God commands him to "ascend to the mountain *and be there.*"[2] Don't we already know that if Moses climbs the mountain, he will "be there"? Why does God add that phrase? What is the Torah telling us?

One early Hasidic master understood the phrase "be there" to teach that "it is possible for Moses to stand on the mountain but for his head to be somewhere else. It is not the physical ascent that is essential; rather what matters is being actively present."[3] Moses is able to receive the Torah because he is able to listen actively, to attend fully to the moment.

In a conversation with his fellow Israelite, Moses demonstrates that important attribute of being present and attentive: being a true leader means taking the time to reflect rather than merely lurching into action thoughtlessly. In the words of the Mishnah, being a leader means "learning from every person."[4] When his father-in-law, Jethro, suggests a better way to govern the Jewish people, Moses adopts it. Thus it is taught that "no one should treat lightly the speech of another. We find that Moses listened attentively to the words of Jethro."[5] When Korah (a priest who resents God's choosing Moses as leader) rebels against the authority of Moses, Korah publicly challenges Moses's right to speak on God's behalf. Confronted before the people, Moses—having spent years performing miracles and having accomplished the liberation of the Israelites from Egyptian bondage—must feel outrage at Korah's sheer arrogance. When Korah finishes speaking, we might expect Moses to reject the rebel's charges. But Moses doesn't blurt out his anger; instead, he pauses, prays, and listens: "When Moses heard this, *he fell on his face*."[6] What is he doing while lying flat on the ground? According to several medieval interpreters, he is listening for God's answer.[7] Only after this silent, attentive gesture does Moses "then speak to Korah and all his company."[8] Moses pauses long enough to listen and understand. During that moment, he gains the levelheadedness and courage necessary to respond effectively.

Both listener and speaker benefit from hearing what the other is trying to say. If we hope to be able to touch another human heart, we must be willing to listen to the outpourings of that heart. When we give the gift of our attention, we open our self to another human being. We grant permission to that other person to be, to grow, and to give in return. In listening, we communicate more than we could ever hope to through speech. Our active listening conveys commitment, closeness, and conviction. We let the recipient—the speaker—know that he or she has found a listening ear, someone willing to take in the pain, joy, doubts, and struggles that meaningful growth requires.

And the listener—what does the attentive listener gain? The *Zohar* teaches that "the heart is the Holy of Holies."[9] There is no Holy Temple today. Its innermost shrine, the Holy of Holies, was the place that witnessed the zenith of holiness in Jewish life. There, in that most sacred of sanctuaries, the most sacred person (the Kohein Gadol, the High Priest) would speak the most sacred word (God's name) on the most sacred day (Yom Kippur, the Day of Atonement). With the destruction of the Temple, we have lost that confluence of sacred place, person, word, and time. But we do have a portal to that fusion of holiness. When we learn to listen to another human soul, we gain access to the place where heaven and earth touch each other: the human heart. Today's Holy of Holies is present wherever two people connect. And connection can happen only if someone is listening.

Four Basic Needs of a Speaker

When speaking with another person, people generally need four things from the listener, in this order:[10]
1. to be heard
2. to feel understood
3. to receive a response
4. to have a sense of closure

If any need is ignored or skipped, the speaker feels cheated. That frustration can interfere with the mentor's ability to teach, counsel, or guide. How do we slow down long enough to let a speaker know that he or she is being heard? How do we follow the advice of the sages to "press your own lips against each other and don't be in a hurry to answer"?[11] And how do we communicate that we understand? To be active listeners, we must work to integrate those four components of listening into how we react when people seek our attention.

The Need to be Heard

Everyone needs to be heard. Sometimes we need to be heard in order to feel affirmed as a person or to feel welcomed as part of a community. Other times the gift of a listening ear can help us sift through conflicting feelings or complicated ideas. You can easily let someone know that you are willing to listen by facing him or her and giving your undivided attention, by turning away from the phone or the computer. Even saying "Please tell me what's on your mind" can offer a haven in a rough and troubling world.

Virtually every student who has attended the Jewish Theological Seminary (JTS) in the past two decades has loved to talk with Rabbi Joseph Brodie. More precisely, those of us who attended JTS in those years loved to talk to Rabbi Brodie because we knew that when we did, we had his undivided attention. As a student spoke, Rabbi Brodie would lean forward in his chair, looking directly at him or her throughout the conversation. Rabbi Brodie's comments encouraged the student to continue speaking, and it was clear from his expression that he understood what the student was feeling. If his phone rang, he ignored it, and he would ask his secretary to prevent interruptions during scheduled meetings. He almost never interrupted when a student was speaking, and if he did, it was to clarify what was said or to inquire about it. In contrast to Rabbi Brodie's attentiveness are listeners who manifest disinterest to demonstrate power, continuing to answer the phone, sign memos, or sift through mail during an appointment. Such negative examples aside, scores of students learned how to offer a listening ear by observing and emulating Rabbi Brodie.

The Need to Feel Understood

When we listen actively, we make possible the fulfillment of the speaker's first basic need: the need to be heard. But that is just a beginning. How do we show that we have not only listened but also understood everything we were told, or at least as much as we were able to understand? Here the essential skill is to paraphrase. It may seem cumbersome and unnecessary, but repeating what we've been told—in our own words—is the only way to guarantee that we didn't distort the message by incorporating our own assumptions and experiences. More important, it shows that we are absorbing what is being said and that we are trying to fit the pieces of the story together in our mind so that we may respond appropriately.

How do we paraphrase in a helpful way? One way is to rephrase a remark as a statement: "So, you mean that . . ." or "In other words . . ." Another approach is to frankly announce the purpose of the paraphrase: "Let me see if I understand what you're telling me. According to you, . . ." Either way, good paraphrasing reworks the speaker's information in the listener's language, letting the speaker evaluate whether the listener's understanding is correct.

The Need to Receive a Response

After actively listening and demonstrating understanding through paraphrasing, a listener must meet the next fundamental need of a speaker: to hear a response. This is every listener's favorite moment: the chance to finally express himself or herself! But beware; it is the speaker's third need, not the first. Only after being listened to and being understood is a speaker ready to hear a response. As difficult as it may be to hold back, restraint is a key ingredient of effective listening. We are told, "Do not intrude upon the speech of your fellow while he is still talking."[12]

Instead of imposing ourselves in a conversation, by saying what we think the speaker is about to say, by responding prematurely, or simply by barging in with our opinion or insight, it's worth waiting to be asked. Once heard and understood, a speaker will want to comprehend the impact of his or her words. The speaker will ask for a response: "So, what do you think?" or "Any take on that?" Once asked, we can expect a far better reception for our opinion since it accommodates the speaker's request. A guest with an invitation is always welcome, at parties and in conversations. Small wonder the ancient experts on dialogue, the rabbis, reminded us, "Do not enter another's home until given permission to enter."[13]

Related to the listener's need to wait for an invitation to speak is the speaker's obligation to wait for an answer when asking a question. Speakers often use questions rhetorically, assuming the listener knows the answer. Instead of letting a disciple feel affirmed and heard, such a rhetorical flourish can lead him or her to feel as if a door had been slammed prematurely.

When someone asks a question, it is important to respond to the question at hand. As the Talmud instructs, "When a student asks something of another student, the latter should answer no more than has been asked."[14] Respond simply. Keep comments to the point. If you are going to disagree, it is more palatable to the listener if you differ with a concrete comment than if you speak generally. If there are reasonable elements in the speaker's erroneous opinion, highlight them first, with appropriate compliments, and then explain why you can't give your consent despite those shared premises. A response is not only an opportunity to speak; it also provides another chance to demonstrate that you have listened.

The Need to Have a Sense of Closure

The speaker's fourth and final need is for closure. After being assured that they have been heard and understood and after receiving a response to what they've said, most speakers will also need to know what to do next. Is there some action that must take place as a result? Is a follow-up conversation necessary? Is there someone else with whom the speaker should talk? All of that must be clarified before the conversation ends. It may be as simple as asking, "So, where does this leave us?" or "Is there something you would like me to do now?" Or it may involve scheduling another meeting: "Let's talk about this again next Thursday at one o'clock." Whatever the nature of the conclusion, it should affirm whatever consensus exists and lay out whatever further action or conversation is necessary and when it will take place.

And the thank you. Every exchange should conclude with thanks for the opportunity to listen and to learn. Even when someone has just complained, it is appropriate to offer thanks. After all, the speaker might have waited for the chance to vent his or her anger or disappointment. (And remember: complaining is an indirect way of maintaining a connection. So it is proper to thank a speaker for trusting you and for caring enough to share the complaint.) Successful conversations, like good sermons or well-organized lesson plans, should have a practical outcome; they should make a difference in the world of both parties.

Feelings

Often what people want to express isn't a piece of information at all; it's a feeling—it may even be a feeling disguised as information ("Let me tell you, Rabbi, that woman can't sing to save her life!"). A significant part of any successful relationship is the expression of feelings. And the proper response to a shared feeling is acknowledgment that the feeling is the speaker's. We don't need to endorse the emotion, nor do we need to repudiate it. Perhaps that's why the Talmud reminds us, "At times, one who keeps silence receives reward."[15]

Why do people share feelings—to affirm their right to respond, to assert their viewpoint, to seek a connection with another person? For whatever reason, when listeners mistake a feeling for a fact, when they jump in with an evaluation or an editorial, they shift the focus of the conversation from where it needs to be instead of simply letting the emotion exist and recognizing it as the speaker's response to a particular situation. When speakers share an emotion, what they most seek is a listening ear and what they need is acceptance. As the Talmud instructs, "Words that come from the heart go to the heart."[16]

Sometimes the feelings a speaker expresses do not require more than an acknowledgment (often through paraphrase): "Sounds like you're pretty angry right now." By defining and restating a person's feelings, the listener signifies to the *talmid* that it is safe to be real, without disguising or distorting the inner self. The listener shows that he or she is willing to stand with the speaker, even in the presence of powerful—often ugly—emotions. And through that display of solidarity, the listener shows that the speaker is not abandoned— not by God, not by his or her heritage, not by the community, not by friends—in moments of pain or rage. Accepting someone's emotions as real, as permissible, is a prerequisite for establishing a sense of trust and involvement. But it need not be the last step. What if the feeling is destructive, erroneous, or hateful? In such instances, accepting that it is how the speaker feels signals the listener's recognition of who the speaker is; it satisfies a person's primal need to be heard and understood. But our obligations to our integrity, to truth, or to the values of Torah require that we also try to help lift our partner—the speaker—above those destructive emotions.

To help listeners reach an understanding of such a feeling, it is essential first to validate the fact that they have the feeling they say they have. But no less crucial is the need to find a loving and supportive way to introduce a different way of feeling. Often that might be accomplished by mentioning that you had a different response to the same situation: "I know you could have heard what he was saying as hateful, but I had a different response. Would you like to hear it?" Sometimes that different perspective is all it takes to allow a protégé to see beyond the trap of his or her pain and fragility. Another possible intervention is to offer new information: "I can see why you find her shallow. But from what I know of her life, it's amazing just how much she has accomplished. May I share some of what I know with you?"

Learning to Speak

Death and life are in the power of the tongue.

—Proverbs

We talk too much.

There are very few of us who weigh our words before blurting out comments we later regret. The first and most difficult lesson of *sh'mirat halashon* (the mitzvah of avoiding malicious speech) is found in its literal translation: we must learn to "guard our tongue." Once uttered, a statement cannot be retracted. Perhaps that is why the ancients compared malicious speech to an arrow released from a bow. The prophet Jeremiah complained, "Their tongue is a deadly arrow,"[17] which the Midrash took to mean that just "as an arrow leaves the bow and injures and kills, so does *l'shon hara* [evil speech]."[18]

A cantor recalled counseling a couple who were contemplating a divorce. They had been married for almost twenty years and had raised three children together. While the tension in their relationship was the result of many complex factors, one comment of the wife's stands out. She confided that she had been able to cope with every disappointment they had faced because she had believed they were part of a team. But one day in his anger, the husband blurted out that he had never been really happy with her. The next morning, he must have realized what he had said, because he told her that he hadn't meant those harsh words, and he presented her with a dozen roses. However sincere his regret, his words shifted the way his wife construed their struggles. No longer did she assume that they were partners committed to resolving shared difficulties, happy to be

together even in tough times. Now she saw herself as lonely and misunderstood. Her love for her husband, she told the cantor, began to
wither that very night. Try as he might, the husband could not retract
his words.

Small wonder, then, that Jewish tradition is sensitive to the harm
that unrestrained speech can inflict. Indeed, an entire category of
Jewish ethical behavior focuses on the need for *sh'mirat halashon* and
the prevention of *l'shon hara*. Several rabbinic sayings and stories, as
well as more recent books, have illuminated this important precept.[19]
Just as learning how to listen is an essential preliminary to serving as
someone's guide and mentor, so, too, is learning how to speak (and
how not to) a crucial task for any would-be mentor. Let us therefore
turn now to that difficult undertaking.

Before specifying useful guidelines for speaking wisely and refraining from speaking ill, let's carve out some common ground with
the assistance of a few definitions. Our concern is not just good manners but a religious context—one that involves the service of God
through nurturing our fellow human beings. Judaism well understands the role that language plays in building a world of wholeness
and holiness. The Bible itself connects well-being to the way in which
we use the gift of speech: "Who is eager for life? Who desires years
of good fortune? Guard your tongue from evil, your lips from deceit-
ful speech."[20] Since speech is a gift from God and one of the defining
traits of human identity, we bear a special duty to use it to further
God's Covenant and holiness in the world.

In explicating the details of that duty, Judaism employs certain
terms and categories that help us consider our proper role as an embodiment of God's gift of language:

• **L'shon hara,** or evil speech, occurs whenever we make a derogatory or harmful statement about a person that does not have a constructive or beneficial goal, regardless of whether it is true or not.
Standing around the water cooler at work and complaining of a

secretary's inability to follow even the simplest instruction and joking in the locker room about a teacher's mannerisms are two examples of this pervasive temptation.

• *Avak l'shon hara,* which literally means "dust of evil speech," occurs when a statement isn't explicitly derogatory but still degrades the one being spoken about in the ears of the listener. Both "I'd tell you where she is going, but it wouldn't be right" and "The less we say about the rabbi's sermons, the better" exemplify this indirect way of belittling someone.

• *Motzi shem ra,* or slander, occurs when information communicated is damaging and false. This is the easiest category to recognize as wrong: speech that is harmful and/or untrue is a lie. The Talmud tells us, "Of those who engage in defamation, the Holy One says, 'It is not possible for such a person and me to dwell in the world together.'"[21]

• *R'chilut,* gossip, is repeating without permission something learned from a third party to the person who is the subject of the statement. This category pertains whether the comment is positive or negative, whether it is true or false. It can range from the clearly harmful "Did you know that Jill thinks you're dumb?" to the more benign "Mr. Smith told me that you are about to receive a promotion. Congratulations!" As innocent as such a remark sounds, the news may be unknown to the person you are telling, untrue, or not yet meant to be made public. As the Talmud teaches, "If silence is good for the wise, how much better must it be for fools?"[22]

Those four categories mark the general parameters of problematic speech. While many sages also urged their followers to eliminate all unnecessary speech, they focused especially on limiting those negative categories. We will focus on them as the basis for developing a pattern and a discipline of speaking that will enable our *talmidim* to know that they can trust us with their secrets, their failings, and their doubts. What we say and what we refuse to repeat are the only proofs of our reliability that we can offer. Without offering that assurance, our knowledge and experience will be of little help to those we seek to guide, since they will not be able to trust us. The path to successful mentoring traverses the portals of *sh'mirat halashon.*

The Art of *Sh'mirat Halashon*: Do Not Speak About Another Person

It's fun to gossip. Whether we're talking about the foibles of public figures or venting about a co-worker in the office, we use gossip as a way to relieve tension, assert a bond, or feel superior. While the vice may be widespread, few other flaws can more quickly cripple our ability to nurture others. Our disciples will notice that we are caustic about the flaws of others and may reasonably assume that in private we are that way about their flaws as well. If they hear us divulging some private matter, they might think that they can't trust us to keep their confidences. And if they participate with us in denigrating someone who is not present, won't they presume that we might speak about them in their absence, too? Or will they fail to learn that such speech is morally unacceptable? While avoiding *l'shon hara* is incumbent on every Jew, it is all the more important for those who seek to assist others.

Jewish tradition offers some clear guidelines to consider prior to offering a comment about someone else. Only if the remark adheres to the following simple standards can we be sure we are using the gift of speech as a blessing:
1. It is the truth.
2. It is necessary—it must be said.
3. It is constructive.
4. It is not duplicitous.
5. It does not repeat a conversation with someone else.

After the fact, if subjected to *l'shon hara,* offer constructive suggestions, change the subject, or leave.

The Art of *Tochaḥah*: Speak Directly to Another Person

A few years ago during one of the perennial cycles of contract renewals that mold the life of a congregational rabbi, a rabbi heard of a congregant who had spoken ill of him at a congregational meeting. He was able to surmount his initial indignation enough to feel the pain that must have motivated the congregant's outburst. The next morning, he phoned the congregant and asked her to meet with him. In a display of remarkable courage and refreshing openness, the woman agreed to the meeting. The two spoke for several hours (actually, the congregant spoke, and the rabbi listened). Toward the end of their time together, the rabbi told her how sorry he was that she had felt ignored and misunderstood and how grateful he was that she had been willing to speak directly to him. Then he asked her to give him a chance to do better. From that day on, the rabbi was able to focus on the congregant's needs and give her the attention that she needed from her rabbi. Their face-to-face conversation had cleared away any hidden animosity and had set a valuable precedent: if either of them had something to say to the other, he or she would say it and then let the other respond directly.

The congregant may not have known it, but her scolding of her rabbi was a mitzvah: the mitzvah of *tochaḥah* (rebuke). The Torah relates the commandment "You shall not hate your kinsfolk in your heart: reprove your kin, but incur no guilt because of your kin."[23] Traditional Jewish commentaries synthesize those two verses to make a larger point: unwillingness to reprove another person is evidence of hating that person. If we care for each other, we must be willing to offer criticism. If we care for each other, we have to believe we can change. Criticism, including self-imposed criticism, induces such changes.

To put it more positively, "Love without criticism is not love."[24] Modern psychology takes as its premise the notion that human emotions do best in the bright light of open discussion and explicit consideration. Feelings denied or buried fester until they emerge in unpredictable and harmful ways. Judaism anticipated that insight when it noted the need for *tochaḥah*—offering reproof to help another person improve—as a way of

> Making for peace and goodness among people. For when one person sins toward another and is reproved in secret, that person will apologize and the other will accept the apology and make peace. But if the other will not offer rebuke, there will be hatred in their hearts and it will cause harm either then or at some other time.[25]

It isn't easy to be able to offer criticism; indeed, constructive criticism is probably the most important and the most difficult gift a mentor can give a *talmid*. A mentor invests time, love, and wisdom because of an abiding faith in the *talmid*'s ability to grow and change. The ideal of a student's renewal and transformation establishes the base on which the mentor's relationship makes sense. As Rebbe Naḥman reminds us, "If you are not going to be a better person tomorrow than you were today, then what need have you for tomorrow?"[26]

Our hope for tomorrow and our faith in each other summon us to undertake the difficult and delicate task of chastisement. The Talmud records a rabbinic seminar on the subject, with three sages offering their insight into the challenges of a proper *tochaḥah*:

> Rabbi Tarfon said, ". . . I doubt if there is anyone in this generation who is fit to rebuke others." Rabbi Elazar ben Azaryah said, ". . . I doubt if there is anyone in this generation who is able to receive rebuke." Rabbi Akiva said, ". . . I doubt if there is anyone in this generation who knows how to rebuke."[27]

We face the daunting challenge of creating an appropriate manner of criticism. We must try to make it possible for the protégé to perceive our criticism as an act of loyalty and love. The burden is on us to make sure that our rebuke is a gift and not an attack. These guidelines can increase the odds that our rebuke will strengthen the relationship, leaving us all in a better position than we were before:

1. Before offering the *tochaḥah*, **make sure you have a willing listener.** It doesn't help to offer a well-considered critical analysis if your listener is unwilling to listen. In fact, it can do significant harm: if the listener can't tolerate criticism or can't tolerate it from you, he or she will construe the critique as an assault rather than a gift. As the book of Proverbs summarizes, "Don't reprove a scoffer, who will hate you for it; reprove a sage who will love you for it."[28] The likely results are a stubborn reiteration of the original mistake as well as an abiding hostility between the two of you. The Talmud speaks well when it insists, "Just as one is commanded to say what will be heeded, so is one commanded not to say what won't be heeded."[29]

2. Before offering *tochaḥah*, **analyze your intentions and feelings.** Rarely are our feelings simple or pure. So when we feel a need to offer *tochachah*, we must first sift through our motivations: will we be acting in a spirit of love and giving, or is an element of jealousy, anger, ambition, or humiliation involved? The goal of a rebuke must be to help the listener do better. If a rebuke isn't rooted in that desire, it's not likely to do much good.

3. When offering the *tochaḥah*, **do it as gently as possible.** According to Maimonides, "One who rebukes another, whether for offenses against the rebuker directly or for sins against God, should administer the rebuke in private, speak to the offender gently and tenderly, and point out that the rebuke is intended only for the wrongdoer's own good."[30] We are serving as mentors when we make it clear at every stage of the process that we are on the *talmid's* side. The manner in which we deliver a rebuke should reveal our love. For that reason, Jewish law prohibits shaming the recipient or persisting when it is clear that no good will come of further chastisement.

4. Offer positive comments and sympathy. Nothing makes criticism easier to accept than a sense that the critic has made a similar mistake, that the erroneous action was not completely unreasonable, or at least that it would have been tempting to anyone in that position. Rabbi Joseph Telushkin offers the example of Rabbi Israel Salanter, the leader of the Musar movement, whose goal was to refocus Jewish piety on inner virtues and ethical purity. Known for his warmth and moral rigor, Rabbi Salanter would announce: "Don't think that I am innocent of all the offenses I am enumerating. I too have committed some of them. All that I am doing, therefore, is speaking aloud to myself, and if anything you might overhear applies to you also, well and good."[31] In presenting himself as in need of the same moral guidance as those he was leading, Rabbi Salanter made it possible for them to accept his comments without feeling diminished or embarrassed. Thus he created a community of people striving to improve together rather than a situation in which one pure soul lectured a community of inferior sinners.

5. Provide reparative steps for rectifying the situation or rebuilding the relationship. Rather than offering an opportunity to take potshots at someone who has erred, the purpose of admonishing a *talmid* is to help him or her improve and live up to the full potential of the divine image within. An important part of *tochaḥah* is providing thoughtful advice on how to repair whatever damage may have already been done. Attending to this crucial (and often ignored) part of a rebuke affirms the love that motivated the intervention in the first place. It also cements the position of the rebuker as ally and mentor. Particularly if the one who was wronged is the one who is offering the chastisement, taking the additional step of suggesting how the situation might be rectified is a clear symbol of a commitment to maintain a positive relationship despite whatever has transpired.

6. Strengthen the relationship. Linked to the last step is the need to explicitly affirm the continuing reality of connection. Whether we are offering *tochaḥah* or receiving it, our boss is still our boss, our colleague still our colleague, our friend still our friend. If it is at all possible, the conclusion of a successful and productive *tochaḥah* ought to be a strengthened connection. Even when that is not possible, when the damage is so total that forgiveness isn't possible, the rebuker can still offer some positive connection as rebuker and rebuked separate, perhaps a reference to the sharing of productive years or a statement that the relationship produced some lasting positive results. The mitzvah of *tochahah* is not a biblically authorized tantrum. Its context and delivery must attest to its expression of service to God's creatures and of loyalty to the One who is regularly expected to forgive and welcome the penitent.

The Art of Silence

The Jewish ethic of speech is to speak to someone, not about someone. But the mitzvah of *sh'mirat halashon* also involves learning how to communicate using silence: "Silence is Your praise."[32] Often words are mere clutter, conspiring to mask our true feelings or evade the significance of the moment; silence can be the best form of communication as it can express the bond two people feel. Once, at a *shiva minyan,* a mourner confided to her cantor that she just wanted to escape her visitors' well-intended chatter. All of their attempts to comfort or distract prevented her from focusing on her feelings, as she desired to do. The cantor sat with her in silence for several minutes. As the time passed, there was a palpable sense of connection between them; others saw them sitting silently on the couch and kept their distance. When the cantor finally got up to leave, the mourner thanked him for being there for her and for not speaking. There are times, then, when only silence can convey the strength and intimacy a moment requires. Often our silent presence is more helpful to mourners and others in pain than anything we might fumble to express in words: "The best medicine of all is silence."[33]

Silence can be the gift of connection. At other times, it is the preferred response because speech would be critical without being constructive. I know of one congregation in which families maintain the practice of printing explanatory booklets at bat and bar mitzvah celebrations. One congregant always scrutinizes the booklets after they have been distributed at services and never fails to let the family know about the typos and other errors that mar their keepsake. There is nothing the family can do at that point except feel bad that their booklet isn't perfect. At such moments, it is doubly true that "if a word is worth one coin, silence is worth two."[34]

There are also times and occasions when speech inflames. As Rabbi Eliezer noted, "Just as with fire, where there is no wood, there is no fire, so where there is no *l'shon hara,* contention ceases."[35] At such moments, silence is truly a fence shielding an emptiness in which healing and caring may flower.

One of the greatest things a human tongue can do is lie still. An attentive mentor listens not only with the ears but also with the heart. Does this protégé need to speak further? Will she be able to hear what I would like to say? Does he need my presence more than any words I might muster? Listening requires more than vibrating eardrums; it involves something deeper. Similarly, the Jewish art of speech involves more than vocalization. Seeking to guide and to nurture, to educate and to inspire, we can use our silence to reach places in the other's soul that our words at best can only evoke. Our charge, then, is to know how and when to speak, sometimes using words and sometimes using only our presence.

A Trick of the Trade

What about those frustrating situations in which someone clearly wants to intrude on a conversation? Everyone is familiar with such moments. During the *oneg* after Shabbat services, every congregational rabbi, cantor, educator, and president is routinely swamped by congregants who need a moment of their time and their undivided attention. So let's play out this conflict. While trying to focus on what Mrs. Goldstein is saying, you see Mr. Blum waiting a few feet away, trying to get your attention. He stares at you, shifting his weight from foot to foot, and loudly clears his throat every few minutes. Mrs. Goldstein knows why he's there and tries to ignore him, which only makes his throat clearing more frequent and louder. You're pretty flustered, too, and find it difficult to attend to Mrs. Goldstein (or to Mr. Blum for that matter). What should you do?

This is an occasion when buying time is a necessity. Somehow you need to tell Mr. Blum that he, too, can have your undivided attention, but he'll have to wait until Mrs. Goldstein is finished. You have to give him this news in a manner that won't offend him, and you have to interrupt Mrs. Goldstein in a way that won't frustrate or belittle her. You want to please both congregants, but something's got to give. The Talmud advises, "Accustom yourself to be pleasant to people,"[36] which is good advice. But how can you be pleasant to two people who are competing for your attention?

Buying time is actually a pretty simple response, and it will work (almost) every time. It consists of four steps, which must be followed in order:

1. Say the name of the person who is waiting.
2. Say something nice.
3. Explain the circumstances.
4. Schedule a time when you can listen to him or her.

As tempting as it may be to simply say "I can't talk now" and return to Mrs. Goldstein (that's part of step 3), it is crucial to begin with step 1. As artificial as this approach may seem, it will become more natural with repetition. All etiquette and every kindness begin as the imitation of someone else's example, the internalization of someone else's standard. When you use this technique, you encourage your personality to grow. You make the buying of time your own technique, and you benefit from its use. Its rewards are so clear and so pleasant that it won't be long before you find yourself sharing this secret with someone else. It won't be long before your reputation as a good listener makes others more receptive to the content of your message.

Let's see how this method might work with Mrs. Goldstein and Mr. Blum. Mrs. Goldstein is telling you how nervous she is about her upcoming surgery. At that point, you both become aware of Mr. Blum, who is swaying and grunting a few feet away. Mrs. Goldstein's speech falters as she becomes distracted. You know that you're not able to focus as you were just a moment before.

"Mrs. Goldstein," you say (perhaps even putting your hand on her arm—if you are reasonably certain your touch will be welcome—to reaffirm your connection), "you know I want to hear about your surgery because you are so important to this community and to me. But it's pretty clear that Mr. Blum wants to talk to me, and I'm finding it hard to hear what you're telling me. Let me tell him when might be a good time for him and me to speak. Then we can continue, and I'll be able to focus." Note well: you used her name, so Mrs. Goldstein knows she's special. You said something nice, so she knows you're not just trying to avoid her. You explained the circumstances to her and finished by guaranteeing when she could continue her conversation with you. Having bought time with Mrs. Goldstein, you now need to go through the four steps with Mr. Blum, using the same pattern: using his name, saying something positive (and true) about him, describing the circumstances, making an arrangement that will satisfy him. Mr. Blum is happy because he knows he's on your list and can expect the same undivided attention when it is his turn to speak. Mrs. Goldstein is happy because she has been complimented and is confidently anticipating your complete attention. You're relieved because you've now created a situation in which you're not torn between competing, frustrated congregants. Everyone emerges a winner.

Buying time isn't just a gimmick. It is a tool for mentors who want to be able to attend to their colleagues, congregants, students, or friends but need a little breathing space in order to be helpful. Those who are mentors—counselors, teachers, role models, or other authorities—will frequently find themselves in this position. Their clients, students, or protégés frequently feel disappointed in the mentor because they sense that they are not being valued or attended to. Buying time allows you to demonstrate your presence, listen with full concentration, and still let others know that you are concerned.

The desire to buy time encourages the omission of the first two steps: after all, Mrs. Goldstein knows that you know her name, and she should know by now that you like her. But without the first two steps, the tone and context become abrupt and harsh. Watch what happens when you simply skip to step 3: you interrupt Mrs. Goldstein's account of her doctor's appointment to say, "Let me tell Mr. Blum when might be a good time for him and me to talk. Then you can continue, and I'll be able to focus." Sounds harsh, doesn't it? Without the assurance that comes from using Mrs. Goldstein's name and giving her a compliment, you sound as though your only concern is your own comfort. Mrs. Goldstein is far more likely to take offense or assume that you do not want to hear what she is telling you.

And Mrs. Goldstein would not be alone in that response. To everyone, the sweetest word in the world is his or her name. So use it. It shows that you recognize and appreciate the person's uniqueness. Once you've made that connection, take the time to say something nice. All people harbor insecurities about themselves, particularly when they think they might be imposing themselves on someone they love or venerate. Offering an assurance that you see some good in them or derive benefit and pleasure from conversation with them will help them tolerate the interruption you're about to impose.

Roadblocks on a Mentor's Path

Chapter Eight

When a Mentor Is Wounded

A Prelude

> *Burden them with the needs of the community, and they*
> *will perish of their own accord.*
>
> —SANHEDRIN

Let me share with you a puzzling and curious Talmudic tale about a third-century sage and a biblical prophet who never died:

> Rabbi Yehoshua ben Levi met Elijah standing by the entrance of the cave of Rabbi Shimon bar Yoḥai's tomb. He asked Elijah, . . . "When will the Messiah come?"
>
> "Go and ask him yourself," was Elijah's reply.
>
> "Where is he sitting?" asked the rabbi.
>
> "At the gate of the city," the prophet replied.
>
> "How may I recognize him?" inquired Rabbi Yehoshua.
>
> Elijah responded, "He is sitting among the diseased poor: all of them untie [their bandages] all at once, and rebandage them together, whereas he unties and rebandages each separately, thinking, I might be needed, I must not be delayed."[1]

In Jewish thought, the Messiah is a human being who will liberate the Jewish people from gentile oppression, regather the Jews into the Land of Israel, and inaugurate a period of universal harmony. Illness, death, brutality, and hatred will vanish during the messianic age. Peace, understanding, and enlightenment will suffuse the globe.

Humanity will unite in the service of the one God, whose Torah will spread from Jerusalem to every corner of the globe. After seeing all this accomplished, the Messiah will transfer the reins of government directly to God, who will unite the living and the dead in an everlasting paradise.[2] Most traditions emphasize the power and glory of the Messiah. Indeed, in a frequent rabbinic usage, the Messiah is called Melech Ha-Mashi'aḥ, Sovereign Messiah.

All the more striking, then, is the humility and poignancy of this Talmudic perspective. Not majestic in pomp but surrounded by the poor and leprous, the Messiah is portrayed as a sovereign in bandages, tending to wounds and pain. The business of the Messiah is caring for those in pain, tending to sores.

Yet the conclusion of the story is ambiguous: we never know definitively whose bandages the Messiah is wrapping. Is the Messiah someone who tends to the wounds of others? Or is the Messiah someone who is wounded? There are authoritative rabbinic sources that read the Talmud both ways. So it becomes a matter of choosing how to read it: the lenses we bring to the story determine whether we see a messiah who serves others or a messiah who both aches and serves. Both visions express important understandings of what a messiah ought to be. And in the end the Messiah is just a mentor at large.

Anyone who would be a mentor will inevitably face the wounds of serving others. Some of those wounds come from the excessive expectations and endless needs of the people served. Some wounds emerge from our limitations and failings, others from the disparity between our aspirations and the reality or between our goals and the willingness of our protégés to engage. And some wounds emerge from the unavoidable conflicts that our jobs and positions create.

Any messiah who seeks to heal will in turn bear wounds. Any mentor who tries to help will enjoy accolades and affection but will also become the object of misunderstanding, desperation, and abuse. Of necessity, being a mentor entails being hurt. The following two chapters offer tools to train successful mentors, mentors who can stay the course and cope with the hurt that inevitably will come.

Chapter Nine

Conflicts Due to a Mentor's Role

> *Moses heard the people weeping throughout their families; everyone in the door of their own tent . . . and Moses was distressed. And Moses said to the ETERNAL ONE, "Why have you dealt ill with your servant. And why have I not enjoyed your favor, that you have laid the burden of all this people upon me . . . I cannot carry this entire people by myself, for it is too much for me. If you would deal thus with me, kill me rather, I beg you, and let me see no more of my wretchedness!"*
>
> — NUMBERS

Any mentor knows great reward and satisfaction: the joy of being able to guide another person to a life of wholeness and holiness, the thrill of steering a shining insight to a new berth, the pleasure of inspiring someone to make a journey of wonder. Yet mentors often pay an excessive price for their labors, sacrificing privacy and time with family and friends.

Built into the fabric of mentorship is the ideal of saintly self-sacrifice. Inspired by a love of God, enflamed with a zeal for the Torah, true mentors are supposed to "sacrifice their very lives in the service of ideas and ideals."[1] Ingrained in the popular mind is a religious person who disdains material comfort and finds fulfillment only in the sublime, the spiritual, and the heroic.[2] Indeed, no less a sage than the great Rabbi Solomon Schechter, in assessing the possibilities for the success of spiritual leadership in his era, offered guarded optimism. He explained that success as a mentor is realized only "provided you are motivated by the spirit which was upon Moses, which is the spirit of self-sacrifice, and giving yourself up entirely to your work."[3] That spirit of sacrifice is a radical, self-assumed denial, indeed: "All this can only be done by young men and women of 'love and strength in superabundance,' forgetting everything, even themselves, and having no other cause at heart but that of [the people of] Israel."[4] The challenge, of course, is that this ideal saint, given up entirely to work, is the expectation not only of the public but also of the mentors themselves. An internalized sense of what a "real" holy man or woman ought to do often fuels the greatest disappointments and senses of failure any mentor might face.

Candidly considering the challenges and tensions that we face shields us from the burnout that the role creates. Taking time for prudent reflection and for the care of family, community, and self can energize our enthusiasm and make it possible to enjoy the many blessings of being a mentor. Scouting out the lay of the land and engaging in advance reflection are valuable endeavors. After all, nothing less than two human souls are at stake: ours and that of the one we serve.

Wounds from the Conflict Between Public and Private Life

Beyond our functions in other people's lives—the lives of those in our community *and* the lives of the members of our family—we are also human beings with interests, needs, and identities of our own. Allocating time and energy among those diverse constituencies and dimensions is a challenge that all mentors face. Congregants, colleagues, and students come to us for guidance and expect us to devote energy and emotion to their struggles. Conflicts emerge as community, family, and self compete for our time and attention.

Consider, for example, Andy, an education director who takes his infant daughter with him when he goes running. He related to me that numerous times when he has been running, pushing his daughter in her stroller, a passing parent whose child attends his school has stopped him to dispute a school policy or investigate an incident in a classroom. Or consider a Federation committee chair who has told me that she shops for groceries only late at night so that she won't be waylaid by a fellow committee member or a grant recipient while she's doing her errands, trying to take care of her family.

In these instances, the individual seeking the mentor's attention isn't necessarily inappropriate. But in these situations, the mentor's seemingly unlimited availability places the role of mentor in direct conflict with his or her need for private time. When the needs of family and community conflict, the burden of maintaining reasonable borders belongs to the mentor. In determining whether our presence is necessary, whether someone else might craft or staff a program, address a problem, or perform a task, or even in recognizing that we are indeed the right person but this is not the right time, we set essential boundaries. Only we, as mentors, can enforce those boundaries. This, too, is Torah, and we must teach it.

It is human nature to seek assistance whenever possible. Indeed, it is human nature to pursue the satisfaction of our needs without limit. If a mentor cannot or will not impose a firm and reasonable boundary, the mentor and those around him or her will suffer. As the Midrash notes, "When the shepherd blunders along his way, his flock blunders after him."[5] Only by maintaining appropriate limits and guidelines is it possible for a mentor to shield family members, preserve private time, and demonstrate how to uphold the Jewish ideals of family and balance.[6]

Creating reasonable boundaries doesn't come easily, especially for people who's nature attracted them to a helping profession in the first place. It took Rabbi Jacobson several years as a congregational rabbi before he was bold enough (or possibly desperate enough) to insist that a congregant who repeatedly phoned him at home during dinner call back at the synagogue during business hours. He recounted the poignant moment when another congregant, in asking for an appointment, said that he could see the rabbi only in the evening because he worked from nine to five. After taking a deep breath, Rabbi Jacobson said, "Me too."

"You too, what?" the congregant asked.

"I also work from nine to five," Rabbi Jacobson responded. "I'd love to meet with you, but it will have to be during business hours." He waited anxiously for an objection or a protest. Remarkably, none followed. The congregant managed to find the time to see his rabbi. In the years that followed, so did every other person who needed to meet with him, just as they would for their doctor or their attorney. Each time he insisted on reasonable hours, he had to muster his resolve. Yet each time, his congregants were willing to accept those limits.

The people we work with can give us permission to be human, with a private life and private commitments, only if we are willing to model that humanity. How can we expect those who seek our guidance to see their identity as more than just their career, how can we encourage them to put their family first, if we ourselves do not? As the Midrash notes, "It is natural that people should imitate their leaders."[7] Our willingness to limit our accessibility is more than self-serving; it is lifesaving for our protégés to be able to imitate mentors who safeguard private time, empowering them to do the same when they begin to serve a community in turn.

Preserving private time isn't an issue just for the mentor; it concerns the members of the mentor's family, too. Colleagues and congregants may feel that the mentor is part of their emotional constellation; hence, protégés often desire to be involved in their mentor's private life—not as an intrusion, but as the natural expression of their love and admiration for their mentor. Often the motivation for those impositions is pure and caring. For example, when my son, Jacob, was diagnosed as having autism, many of my congregants came forward to offer helpful information and deep compassion. Their concern and care were truly healing and comforting to my family. In fact, we are eternally indebted to one courageous congregant who was willing to encourage us to seek a diagnosis. But sometimes the special scrutiny that the mentor's family may be subject to can place an unfair burden on the spouse and children simply because the community members feel that the mentor is theirs and hence the mentor's family is theirs, too. Because the mentor is seen as an embodiment of idealized holiness and righteousness, the mentor's spouse and children are expected to adhere to that standard as well. For example, a cantor's daughter recalled that people would stare at her during worship services, expecting her (unlike all her other peers) to have memorized the entire liturgy (and to sit quietly—and interminable!—in her seat) simply because her father was a cantor. Creating reasonable boundaries so that sharing remains mutual and beneficial is essential if mentors and protégés are to bless each other's lives with goodness.

The conflict between public and private life extends beyond the needs of family, encompassing the mentor's personal needs as well. If all that mentors do is give to others, they can easily wind up tired, depleted, and resentful. There is no less a conflict than that between the mentor's personal needs as an individual and the expectations that others may have of them (fairly or not).

Think of the typical schedule of a congregational rabbi as an example: In the morning, minyan at 7:00 or 7:30, perhaps an early class, hospital visits, community meetings, public presentations, counseling, fund-raising. In the afternoon, meetings with bar and bat mitzvah students and families and teaching in the Hebrew school. In the evening, adult education, committee and board meetings, and introduction-to-Judaism programs. Somewhere in the midst of all the bustle, the rabbi has to find time to do research; to write sermons, Torah commentaries, and bulletin articles; to respond to correspondence and answer phone calls. The relentless pressure is not confined to the workweek of the secular world: all congregational rabbis work at least six days a week, and many work seven (on Shabbat, there are services and bar and bat mitzvah celebrations; on Sunday, there is Hebrew school, and there might also be weddings, funerals, unveilings, community events, and other obligations). There just isn't a lot of time left over for personal and family needs. A similar schedule would describe the lives of cantors, educators, agency executives, and the valiant volunteer leaders who make Jewish community possible.

Being a mentor may mean sacrificing personal time for the sake of one's flock. One night at the end of a particularly exhausting conference, Sam, the president of his local chapter of the Bureau of Jewish Education, was anticipating the closing plenary session with relish; finally, he would go home and get some much-needed sleep. A beloved fellow officer approached and said, "Sam, you look really tired. You shouldn't work so hard. You should go home." As he thanked her for noticing and was about to head for the door, she continued, "Sam, before you go home, I need just five minutes of your time. I need to tell you about something we're planning to request for next year's budget."

With each congregant or student looking to satisfy his or her needs, it is all too easy for mentors to feel that the demand for their time and attention is a burden. Straining to show patience and understanding, a mentor can feel overwhelmed and depleted. Small wonder that the medieval *Sefer Ḥasidim* says, "When people do not appreciate a good leader, they get a wicked one instead."[8]

One simple tool that can strengthen the resolve to maintain balance is to recognize that it is a biblical commandment to care about yourself no less than you care for others. How striking that the mitzvah impels you to "love your fellow as yourself."[9] Why doesn't the Bible simply instruct us to love our fellow? Why does God add those telling two words: "as yourself?" Many mentors are too willing to grant a higher priority to the needs of others than to their own. So they cancel a workout to squeeze in one more meeting or one extra assignment. They stay up late attending yet another community function or take work home rather than spend the evening communing with a loved one or just enjoying time alone. Perhaps that is why we need to be instructed: we must not love others more than we love ourselves.

Indeed, if we do not love ourselves enough, we will soon become incapable of loving our fellows. Without attending to our health (through regular exercise, a healthful diet, and adequate sleep) and without nurturing our spiritual growth (by taking the time for study, contemplation, and fun) we will have little of value to offer anyone else. Two thousand years ago a great sage observed: "Why do sages die before their time? Not because they are adulterers or thieves but because they do not take care of themselves."[10] It is a religious imperative to satisfy our basic personal needs no less than we would satisfy the needs of those people in our care.

Caring for our needs will sometimes, unfortunately and unavoidably, necessitate our inability to meet the needs of another. How essential, then, to admit that every task will not get finished, every goal will not be met. And that is okay. Perfection pertains only to God. God's servants must be (and can be) satisfied with something less. "Good enough" is a reasonable goal for parents and, indeed, for mentors, too.

Our role model for this practiced withdrawal is none other than God. Recall the model presented in Chapter 3, of God withdrawing in an act of *tzimtzum* to make space for everything else. So, too, with the leadership of a mentor: if we don't withdraw, our community will never know what it can accomplish on its own. It is a consummate act of *imitatio Dei,* imitating God, for a mentor to lead selectively. And such engaged withdrawal also provides time for a mentor to savor his or her private life.

Wounds from the Intrinsic Strains of the Position

Many mentors begin their service far from the people who served them as mentors and who constituted their community, a circumstance that can induce one of the first strains of mentorship. I remember an associate whose first pulpit was in Kentucky. The congregation was in a beautiful suburban community. Yet my associate's joy at living in such an idyllic and friendly community was somewhat diminished by her distance from her family (in Boston) and from the Los Angeles community that had nurtured her Jewish life for the previous several years. Now, nearly a continent away from her school and her teachers, those who had been on hand to answer her questions and prompt her growth were accessible only by phone.

For the first several years in Kentucky, she found herself in the odd position of knowing exactly which store in Boston carried the items she needed at any given moment but not having the faintest idea where to find them in Kentucky. The magnificent libraries of California and the Northeast that house so much Judaica were now beyond her reach. Instantly, her meager collection of books became the grand Jewish library of Kentucky. Often she knew exactly which friend she wanted to meet for lunch, or she longed to share a cup of coffee with her sisters, only to realize that her network for care and support was far away. While her years in the congregation brought her new experiences, new friends, and new insights, she never ceased yearning—for the mentors who had nurtured her as a student or for her extended family. The disruption and distance are a price paid by almost every mentor, volunteer, or professional who ventures outside an established community of Jewish learning.

That desire to remain in close contact with a network of mentors may have inspired a very different tale of connection, this one from the Mishnah:

> Rabbi Yosei ben Kismah said, "Once I was traveling on a journey. A certain man met me and extended greetings. I greeted him in return. He asked, 'Where are you from?' I replied, 'I come from a great city of sages and scribes.' He said, 'Rabbi, if it would please you to live with us in our community, I would give you thousands of gold *dinarim*, as well as the most precious stones and pearls in the world.' I replied,

'Though you give me all the silver, gold, precious stones, and pearls in the world, I would not live anywhere except in a community with [teachers of] Torah.'"[11]

This longing for belonging is common to cantors whose teachers and those who serve as their professional inspiration now live far away, to educators who serve in far-flung schools, and to lay leaders whose annual conventions allow them to maintain helpful connections with central organizations and fellow leaders (the communities of the Young Leadership Cabinet[12] and the Wexner Heritage Foundation[13] are examples of intense communities that assemble only periodically). Isolated in their communities, mentors can occasionally feel like outsiders. The key to overcoming that feeling is understanding that everyone, mentors included, needs mentoring. Having the opportunity to be replenished can allow a mentor to reconnect with the passion and caring that mentorship makes possible. It becomes easy to feel cut off from sources of spiritual, intellectual, and professional nourishment and growth if one is only on the mentoring side of life. As in other relationships, mutuality is crucial, and finding ways to feel nurtured is the road to renewed delight in one's students and protégés.

Coping with distance from peers, from one's community, from teachers and learning is an ongoing challenge for any mentor. For those who feel that void, creating a suitable response can spell the difference between a fruitful and satisfying career and one that simply passes time. For some of us, that might mean taking frequent trips to visit the people and places that provide the necessary refreshment. Sometimes making time for a phone call (or a letter or an e-mail message) can make a difference in how lonely or depleted one feels. Finally, educating communities about the importance of providing their mentor with opportunities to grow, relax, and rejuvenate is a way of making sure that mentors will continue to love their tasks and their community. For example, a community might encourage its leaders to attend conventions and seminars, both for the collegiality and for the opportunity to study and learn. This cannot be stressed enough: leaders need time to gather with colleagues to contemplate and revise their vision and their priorities. Mentors need to connect with their own mentors to continue to have the inner resiliency to help nurture their charges. At times, a mentor needs the care that only other mentors can offer.

A second form of isolation stems from the shortage of time—time to reflect, to learn, and to think about the next move. Inevitably the endless stress of being a mentor reduces the moments spent in quiet contemplation and time for advanced preparation. A midrash interprets the biblical verse "I went down into the garden of nuts".[14]

> Resh Lakish said, "The nut tree is smooth. Anyone who would climb to its top without considering how to do it is sure to fall to his death, thus taking his punishment from the tree. So, too, one who would exercise authority over a Jewish community without considering how to do it is sure to fall and take his punishment from the hands of the community."[15]

How often does an agency president get the time to analyze the needs of the community that the agency serves; how often does he or she have the luxury to reflect on the agency's long-term needs and responses? I know of a director of a Hebrew school who is so consumed with supervision and the daily tasks of running the school that preparation for a long-term vision must be delegated to volunteers and outside experts! How many cantors are so pressed by the daily round of bar and bat mitzvah preparations, sick visits, and classroom sessions teaching basic Jewish songs and prayers that they have precious little time for learning new compositions, mastering more complex liturgical renditions, or considering how to renew synagogue worship? Most synagogue presidents and board members similarly report that they are overwhelmed by the daily tasks of their position and have little time left in which to focus on the big picture.

The consequences of not providing time for adequate reflection and planning can be enormous. In his excellent study of leadership, Professor Ronald Heifetz spoke of the need for a leader to make time to reflect and assess his or her perspective. The image he used is of watching a dance from an elevated position: "To discern the larger patterns on the dance floor—to see who is dancing with whom, in what groups, in what location, and who is sitting out which kind of dance—we have to stop moving and get to the balcony."[16]

Only by making time to reflect can we turn our vision to the larger picture. Only by stepping away can we focus our attention on the underlying dynamics and the unarticulated cries. Yet time to contemplate is hard to come by and always seems expendable. In the press of daily crises and filled schedules, reflection and contemplation (not to mention time for renewal) seem like luxuries. One of the few approaches that has helped me make time for growth and reflection has been to make it a requirement.[17] If there is a subject you want to learn more about, offer to teach it as a course or make yourself a syllabus, and become your own teacher-disciplinarian. This pertains to people who teach in classrooms, and to those who teach by example or in informal settings. I know of one determined rabbi who schedules four two-day retreats for himself throughout the year. He describes those retreats as his lifeline.

Clinging to a lifeline becomes all the more important because of the frequency with which leaders and mentors have to absorb other people's agendas, tensions, and anger. Mentors, by virtue of teaching about matters of soul and community, are often the first people someone in need turns to for counsel. Accounts of the inevitable tensions among members of a community often find their way to a mentor's ear, often with an expectation that the mentor will sympathize and intervene on behalf of one party over the other. One of the most difficult aspects of being a good mentor is dealing with situations in which people bring their disappointment or anger to their mentor (sometimes without even realizing it), leaving the mentor to deal with the excess rage, despair, and alienation.

An executive director of a Jewish institution reported that when the terms of her new contract were made public, a board member approached her and said, "I respect you. But my husband doesn't earn that kind of money, so why should you?" Another self-professed supporter told her that the proposed term of service was too long. Yet another informed her that he had opposed the renewal of her contract because of his hatred of the agency president, the chief lay leader who had negotiated the contract. "Nothing personal," said the disgruntled agency volunteer, "but I didn't know how else to send a message."

Executive directors are far from the only mentors who absorb other people's venom. Educators, teachers, rabbis, Jewish professionals, and lay leaders get clobbered daily, sometimes deliberately and often as a simple manifestation of pain, jealousy, or weakness. In one case, a rumor flew through a Jewish day school that the wife of the principal was a lesbian. When he was finally able to locate the source of the gossip, the principal discovered it to be a parent of one of the school children whose spouse had died several years earlier. The widower's response to his overwhelming loneliness was a misplaced bitterness. At a lecture, he had seen the principal's wife sitting next to another woman, decided that they must be lovers, and spread the notion that the principal was inappropriate for his position because of his wife's sexuality!

In another example, a cantor's husband suffered such a debilitating illness that he required constant attention and assistance with visits to doctors, meal preparation, and a variety of other chores. The cantor worked hard at the synagogue while trying to keep up at home. A few congregants offered to help and set up a schedule for members of the synagogue to take turns bringing and serving meals, assisting with some of the household tasks, and transporting the husband to and from his medical appointments. Throughout the long months of his illness, the cantor was awake late into the night tending to her husband. During the day, she was frantically completing her work so that she could get home and manage her household obligations. One day a congregant came to her home to prepare a meal. The cantor, about to take a much-needed break, sat down with the morning newspaper. The next day congregants who had previously volunteered to help called to cancel. Why? The congregant who was there when the cantor took her break had told them that the cantor didn't need the help since "she lounged around the whole time I was there."

Responding

With the mantle of mentoring come situations in which protégés shift deep feelings about others to the mentor. They do this, usually unintentionally, as a way to get someone who appears wiser or more powerful than they to resolve a primal issue, to test the mentor's love and steadfastness, or simply to scream for help. Psychologists recognize this as transference, which may be defined as an "unconscious phenomenon in which the feelings, attitudes, and wishes originally linked with important figures in one's early life are projected onto others who have come to represent them in current life."[18] Often people respond to a mentor as a stand-in for a parent, spouse, teacher, or other powerful figure from an earlier phase of their life. As mentors, we can develop strategies to respond to the redirected emotions and disproportionate anger or affection of the members of our communities. To ensure our well-being and our ability to be of service to others, we *must* clarify these strategies.

On a practical level, that effort means establishing ways to protect oneself and deflect the excessive emotion. The protective response can entail leaving time for a walk or a workout after "public" time. Or it can mean having a book of poetry handy to help one regain focus after a difficult encounter (I rely on the book of Psalms). Or again, it can mean a quick phone call to a loved one (or one's mentor) just to hear an assuring and loving voice.

In the distinct and nonreciprocal way in which mentors and the people they nurture relate, negotiating the welter of personal feelings can be complicated and painful on both sides. However close the relationship may seem (and the love between mentor and protégé is deep and abiding), it is essential for the mentor to remember that the premise of the relationship is serving the other. Unlike a simple friendship, which is explicitly reciprocal, the initial terms of a mentoring relationship involve the mentor's serving the other person. That unequal connection never completely recedes.

And as mentors, we must retain our humility. Recognizing that we serve God allows us to refrain from trying to *be* God (a hopeless task if ever there were one!). Awareness of our limitations helps us allocate our resources and attend to the most important or pressing tasks while empowering others to shoulder the rest.

Chapter Ten

When Expectations and Reality Clash

When I called, you did not answer,
When I spoke, you would not listen.
You did what I hold evil,
And chose what I do not want.

—ISAIAH

Not every conflict a mentor experiences results from an attempt to balance private and public needs or even from the pressures of being a spiritual guide and mentor. Some of the most intense challenges spring from a gap between one's fondest ambitions and the prosaic reality. Seeking to inspire a community to act with greater vitality and effectiveness, enthusiastic lay leaders and new professionals may throw themselves into their work only to find that the members of the community are content with the way things are. Even more difficult, institutions are sometimes resistant to significant change. Bursting with new ideas, a lay leader may join a committee only to find its other members indifferent and hostile to innovation. All too often, such a mentor enters the scene inspired by what might be and is met by a stultifying commitment to what is.

Related to the excessive expectations of a would-be mentor are the human limitations of any mentor or leader. Even if the members of the community are willing to stretch, to grow along the lines proposed by the mentor, the vastness of the task can overwhelm the mentor, and an overwhelmed mentor is likely to focus on his or her limitations and weaknesses.

Sometimes the very devotion of one's protégés creates a problem—an unrealistic sense of entitlement on the part of the student. A popular cantor I know leads services that attract several hundred people each Shabbat. Yet he once received an irate call from a congregant: "Cantor," the man said, "I've not been at services the last three weeks, and you haven't even called to find out why!"

Because people feel a profound and lasting bond with their mentor, they may feel deeply hurt when that bond isn't reciprocated immediately or according to their own terms. Once a friend of mine was distraught with his congregation's rabbi. My friend's mother, a member of another synagogue, had just passed away, and his rabbi was out of the country, on his annual vacation with his family. My friend had phoned the rabbi (in Europe!), insisting that he return to conduct the funeral service. He was outraged because the rabbi would not interrupt his vacation on his congregant's behalf.

In such instances, a conflict erupts because of unrealistic expectations of intimacy. Precisely because the mentor has been effective in shaping the protégé's spiritual development, in guiding his or her life, the protégé feels a sense of intimacy with the mentor that is quite different from the emotion felt by the mentor. In this regard, leaders and mentors share a common context with psychotherapists. However intense the client-therapist relationship may be, it is bounded by the benefit accruing to the client. Because the relationship isn't symmetrical, with information about personal issues flowing in both directions, the expectations that emerge are not identical. To some extent, the challenge that results is an inevitable product of being an effective mentor.

The best way to handle unrealistic personal expectations is to bring subconscious feelings to the light of conscious discussion.[1] Verbalizing unexpressed emotions might make it possible to discuss them in a reasonable and balanced way. If a protégé feels brushed aside, a discussion of the tasks the mentor must balance and the ways in which the relationship is precious can help restore a sense of care that the mentor feels for the protégé. A mentor's relationship with a student, congregant, colleague, or client is different from his or her relationship with family members or friends, yet it is still precious. It has a quality all its own, one that is different from the contours of more private connections. An affirmation of the joy and strength the mentor derives from the relationship, coupled with a straightforward assertion of the mentor's need for a private life (protected from his or her communal role) can validate the seeker's sense of worth while providing him or her with a reality check. Armed with sufficient data and accurate information, both individuals involved in the mentoring relationship have the option to adjust to the situation. Such openness may not eliminate all disappointment or resentment. And it certainly won't appease someone with an unhealthy dependence or a mentor with a needy ego. But it does preserve the reliability of both the mentor and the person being served, allowing them to interact as allies honest enough to navigate nuanced truths and the complexity of their relationship.

When Difficult Situations Arise

Remember: leaders and mentors need time off, too. A religious-school teacher told of meeting some students and their parents on the beach one Sunday in Florida. He thought nothing of it until the middle of the week, when he was summoned to the synagogue office. Sitting there were the synagogue president, vice president, and education trustee. They informed the teacher that they considered him a role model of Judaism and that it was inappropriate for his students to see him in a swimsuit.

Just as the one being mentored needs a confidential forum in which to explore spiritual growth, moral rigor, and intellectual complexity, so, too, does the mentor need to be able to express the fullness of his or her humanity without worrying about the impact of that humanity on the community's idealization of its mentor. Clearly there are limits to the sense of time off. The truth is that being a spiritual leader and mentor is a full-time calling. At all times and in all places, people will look to the mentor as a role model. So actions that violate the mentor's core principles—behavior that is immoral, cynical, or degrading—is always off limits (as it should be for everyone). But that caveat does not diminish the fact that a mentor needs times and places in which to be himself or herself. The need for time off is a healthy counterbalance to a strong desire to make a positive difference in the world and help others live better lives.

Positioning ourselves as helpers, leaders, and mentors often exaggerates our capacity to help, and we may consequently feel frustrated and even put upon when our assistance doesn't solve a problem. As the Midrash understands it, once you assume a leadership position, "you put yourself in the arena. And one who is in the arena is either conquered or conquers."[2]

Joel, the president of a large synagogue in the Northwest, told me that two of the most prominent board members in his congregation had ended a close friendship. Since Joel was a good friend of both of them (he had been the one to get them involved in the synagogue in the first place) and since he knew that their rift would strain the congregation, he decided to intervene. Long hours of separate meetings ensued as the valiant president attempted to find a path that would lead the two to reconcile. Yet their enmity proved greater than Joel's time and energy. First one and then the other quit the board, each accusing the board of siding with his enemy. And Joel? His first response was anger with the two of them for not listening to him. His friendship with each became brittle as he felt their refusal to reconcile constituted a rejection of his needs and interests. Over time, his friendship with each disputant eroded completely. But Joel's next response was equally tragic. His failure to bring the two men together gnawed at him, slowly eroding his confidence in his leadership. As Joel focused on what he had not been able to do, his attention to pressing board matters diminished. He grew increasingly aware of what he could not accomplish and quit his post a year before the completion of his term.

Joel's experience is not unique. We all know of times when we are either called on or feel called on to solve a problem that is simply bigger than we can handle. Or we are presented with a problem that has no solution. Rather than returning responsibility to its proper location, we agree to shoulder it ourselves. As a chaplain at the Memorial Sloan-Kettering Cancer Center in New York City, I often spoke with patients whose cancer was in its most advanced stage. Nothing I said or did would alter the course of the disease or restore their health. Their sorrow and grief were appropriate to the circumstances of their lives. That inability to cure or cheer often debilitated me, as it does so many mentors in similar circumstances. When our intervention fails to make the problem go away, we see it as a devastating flaw in our ability to lead.

In that sense, we are often our own worst critics. The art of leadership requires knowing when to intervene, how to intervene, and how to assess the limits of one's capacity. Rabbi Abraham Joshua Heschel summed up an important strand of mystical thought when he wrote, "An architect of hidden worlds, every pious Jew is, partly, the Messiah." [3] What is true and elevating as a mystical metaphor is erroneous and dangerous as psychological myopia: we often view ourselves as messianic, at our peril. Being a mentor is not the same as being a messiah. There are problems we cannot solve. We serve at our best when we accept our finitude and fallibility. A willingness to remain with someone during a tragedy we cannot avert is one of the greatest gifts we can bestow. When we show solidarity with a dying patient, we allow him or her to face reality with a sense of community, purpose, and connection intact. By admitting our limitations, we testify to our faith in God; since God is God, we are free to be merely human.

Dealing with Ambivalence

Mentors are consistently challenged by the fundamental ambivalence of many Jewish people toward their religion. How many Conservative rabbis are told by new members that they joined the congregation because the Orthodox synagogue "is too Jewish" and the Reform synagogue "isn't Jewish enough"? How many Jews explain their choice of a Reform synagogue by saying that they are "not religious" (or, worse, "not very Jewish")? How many Jews who join an Orthodox synagogue are motivated by nostalgia or habit? So many Jews measure their Judaism by the same standards that the three bears used to assess the porridge of Goldilocks! I know one Reform educator who was encouraged to offer more adult education courses on fundamental Jewish beliefs and practices. At the end of a passionate presentation on the laws of kashrut, a congregant (who had asked for the series) told the educator that he loved the values that kashrut embodied but believed that in the modern world such practices just didn't make sense.

Endless examples confirm the same point: many, many Jews today have deeply mixed feelings about their Jewishness. They are simultaneously drawn to Judaism's beauty, wisdom, and ability to connect Jews across the generations and afraid of losing their independence, their freedom of thought, or even their social status. Such Jews are not hostile to Judaism. What they are is ambivalent. They desire more Judaism, yet they flee from it.

Being a mentor to a community of people who feel such profound ambivalence can be debilitating. My colleague Ron Wolfson of the Fingerhut School of Education at the University of Judaism calls "carpool tunnel vision" the phenomenon of parents' dropping off their children at Hebrew school without ever leaving their car and going inside to find out what it is their children are studying. If being a mentor means sharing our passion for Jews and Judaism, if it means opening our lives to our followers and colleagues, then how can we mentor people who both desire and disdain the Judaism we offer? And how can a mentor share his or her life with people who may admire the life but do not want to share in it?

While it is easy to become disheartened and focused on the ambivalence, it is crucial for the mentor to be able to view her or his community members from their perspective. Even when they don't rise to the level of observance or passion that the mentor would desire, their growth does meet a profound human need; if it didn't, they wouldn't be participating at all. One of the challenges of soul work is that it resists quantification: one never can measure the difference one makes. A rabbi once related to me that he was surprised when a congregant told him that he, the rabbi, had broken through the congregant's depression and loneliness by approaching him at a Saturday-morning service and offering him a *tallit*. The man put on the *tallit* and felt as though his rabbi were embracing him on behalf of the entire community. For him, the experience was a transformative affirmation. He still didn't attend services regularly, but whenever the rabbi ran into him, his affection was real and intense.

As mentors, we need to remind ourselves to measure success using primarily the standards of the heart, not those of the economist (the budget) or the pollster (attendance sheets and membership rosters). When a mentor transcends the standards of evaluation used in the social sciences, he or she is simply affirming an old religious truth that spiritual and ethical advances must be measured by a different yardstick.

Related to the strain of wrestling with the persistent ambivalence of our community is the challenge of discovering that even our "successes" do not yet rise to the level we desired or expected. A knowledgeable synagogue volunteer in the Midwest told me of two close friends of hers who are also members of her congregation. They took her "Introduction to Judaism" class and were delighted to discover the rich spirituality and disciplined path of holiness that Judaism offers. After her class on kashrut, they announced to their friend that they intended to keep kosher. After the session on Shabbat, they told her that they were also going to take Shabbat more seriously. From that day on, these congregants didn't miss a Saturday-morning service. One Shabbat, however, while walking home, the teacher saw her friends outside a nonkosher butcher, loading shopping bags full of meat (purchased on Shabbat no less!) into their car. Again, it needs to be said that these were congregants who had grown tremendously in their observance of both kashrut and Shabbat. They were regulars, attending services week after week. The point is *not* that they weren't taking their Judaism seriously. In fact, their level of observance was far greater than it had been previously and was far greater than that of their relatives. Nevertheless, what they meant by taking Judaism seriously and what the teacher meant by taking it seriously remained quite distinct.

Such a gap exists in every denomination and every arena. Board officers experience a gap when they are disappointed by the amount of time or money their committee members are willing to volunteer or donate. Educators feel frustrated and irrelevant when they are confronted with a lack of parental involvement or support. Leaders of Jewish agencies feel discouraged when their members fail to become passionate about the key issues that their agency addresses; they can't understand why members go out of their way to join the organization but also seem to go out of their way to avoid involvement in it.

Handling Indifference

Unfortunately, a lack of involvement by *talmidim* can easily lead to a lack of appreciation for a mentor's devotion and efforts. Helaine was the chair of her synagogue's ritual committee for six years. Throughout each year, she fielded members' complaints and suggestions about the nature of the service and the participation of the rabbi and cantor. Her duties were manageable, although she missed the sense of an oasis that she had formerly derived from synagogue worship. During the summer, her life became truly hectic. Those were the months she spent arranging the services for the Days of Awe, determining who would receive which honor, who would sit where, who would read which part. The summer days were quickly lost to an endless series of details to arrange and people to contact. Somehow each year she managed to pull together the services, yet each year had its inevitable pitfalls: the occasional detail that she simply missed, the people who did not show up to meet the obligation of their honor, the people who were offended by the honor they were given. After six devoted years, she passed on the leadership of the committee to another congregant. And on the next Rosh Hashanah and Yom Kippur, she wasn't given so much as a single honor. No thank-you letter for her years of service, no note of thanks from the board. Helaine felt that she had slipped into the depths unnoticed. At first, she felt sad and neglected. Gradually her sorrow shifted to anger: she felt used by the community. Within a few months, Helaine was finding it impossible to attend services without feeling rage at the community. By the next Rosh Hashanah, she was no longer a member of the synagogue.

Helaine's sense of being used is all too common in the Jewish community. While no simple solution is at hand, we all need to be zealous in giving tribute where it is due, in scouting for signs of fatigue or resentment in the leaders of our synagogues, schools, organizations, and community centers. If we can intervene before exhaustion overwhelms, before rage erupts, we can provide an overworked mentor with healing, and we can stimulate the progress of the community. In this instance, involving our colleagues is the best guarantee that someone will be there when we grow weary or feel oppressed by our tasks.

We must also remember that the relationship between a mentor and a community should be mutually satisfactory. In other words, the personality (goals, preferences, and levels of enthusiasm) of both parties must match. Sometimes, though, the challenge to the mentor is precisely one of mismatched personalities. Not every mentor can shine in every community. Just as a successful match of spouses takes finding two personalities that accommodate and accept each other in style, values, and needs, so, too, with mentors and their community. For example, Jim graduated from rabbinical school and went straight to a small congregation in New Jersey. The membership was elderly, and while the synagogue wasn't losing members, it wasn't growing either. Jim was an enthusiastic young rabbi with a strong creative streak. He would compose poems for the synagogue bulletin and create innovative worship services that blended meditation and music—his talent had made him popular with his classmates in rabbinical school. Yet at the first creative service in his new congregation, the congregants sat mutely, not reacting to the service at all. When it was over, the shul president approached Jim and said, "Well, I hope we won't see too much more of that!" Jim's experience went downhill from there. If he used slang, congregants would write letters of complaint to the chair of the ritual committee. If he showed up at work without a tie, they would comment. Fewer and fewer people showed up for his services or his classes. At the end of his second year, Jim took a job at a new synagogue in Florida. The members were primarily young families, and the congregation had a booming preschool. Jim was a hit: congregants loved his humor, his energy, his irreverence, and his informality. Everything that struck out in New Jersey made him beloved in Florida. Jim has remained at the Florida pulpit to this day. And the New Jersey congregation found an older rabbi eager to work part-time, whose gentle love of the seniors has made him a beloved leader in a community that now feels appreciated.

There are times when the best response, for the leader and the community, is for the leader to leave. After honest soul searching, after facing the possibility that the *talmidim* are offering legitimate criticisms, it may well be that the mentor and the institution are simply mismatched. It is no mitzvah to stubbornly stay at a place where one's strengths are not needed and one's weaknesses might do damage. The Torah offers guidance in the experience of Abraham and Lot: "Now Abram was very rich in cattle, silver and gold. . . .

Lot, who went with Abram, also had flocks and herds and tents, so that the land could not support them staying together . . . and there was quarreling between the herdsmen of Abram's cattle and those of Lot's cattle."[4] Although linked by ties of affection and family, their "partnership" degenerated into open hostility and sniping at each other's wealth and staff. Rather than insisting on staying together and exacerbating the conflict, Abraham had the wisdom to recognize that their relationship would improve if they no longer lived and worked together: "Abram said to Lot, Let there be no strife between you and me, between my herdsmen and yours, for we are kinsmen. Is not the whole land before you? Let us separate; if you go north, I will go south; and if you go south, I will go north."[5]

Sometimes the path to healing leads us away from the site of the conflict. Disengaging from antagonists or situations that merely accentuate differences can be a mark of wisdom. Moving can itself be a tool of leadership, permitting a community or a mentor to reclaim strengths, recover from a bruising relationship, or move past an error in judgment.

In the end, moving proved to be the best remaining solution for one capable professional: Eleanor took a position as executive director of a struggling Jewish Community Center (JCC). Her confidence, warmth, and energy attracted the board members to hire her, and they were convinced that she had the skills needed to turn their JCC around. At first, Eleanor threw herself into the task with abandon. No chore was too petty or consuming, no subcommittee met without her being present, and if no one else volunteered, she would step in and accept additional obligations. Within a year, the JCC membership was growing (for the first time in years), yet there were fewer volunteers than before, and the budget was just as strained. Eleanor was falling behind in her work but putting in long days six days a week. Her board members praised her for always being at the center—she would be stuffing envelopes, making posters, phoning committee members to confirm meetings, setting up luncheons, and doing all the other chores that previously had been left to volunteers. Eventually, wearing thin from the weight of all those tasks, Eleanor met with the JCC officers and complained that she needed more staff members or volunteers to do the work. She explained that she had to put in far too many hours and was wearing herself out. While the officers expressed both sympathy and gratitude, they were keenly aware that their budget didn't allow for additional staff, and they had grown used to Eleanor's taking care of everything. But they agreed to try to find more volunteers. Each announcement for a volunteer was met with a short-lived response. The JCC president and board members were aware of their debt to Eleanor and frequently complimented her, in private and in public. A year and a half into the job, Eleanor announced that she would resign at the end of the fiscal year. Her mood was grim, and her anger was palpable. She felt that the lay leaders had betrayed her, lauding her yet failing to provide real assistance in terms of staff, resources, and involvement.

Here it must be noted that the failure encompassed both parties. While it is true that the lay leadership had not provided Eleanor with a proper work environment and staff for the tasks at hand, and had not made it their priority to keep open lines of communication with her to preclude such an institutional failure, Eleanor also carries some of the burden for the end result. Eleanor, as a mentor and leader, had an obligation not merely to get the job done. She also had an obligation to construe her responsibilities more broadly. By taking on the duties of her staff members and lay leaders for such a long time, Eleanor virtually guaranteed that they would not be able to share responsibility with her, even after she realized that she could not do all the work herself. A true leader is one who mobilizes his or her lay leadership and community. Had Eleanor realized that, she might have been less inclined to finish every project herself, because she would have been able to see that doing so was precisely the wrong response. Leading—being a mentor—cannot mean that one's protégés don't have any hard work to do. Indeed, making it possible for them to do the hard work may be the single most important gift a mentor can offer.

An ancient Midrash relates a tale in praise of a Rabbi Yehudah ha-Nasi (Rabbi Judah the Prince) that serves today as a warning against burnout. So great was the need of the members of the community to present their problems to him that the moment he emerged from the public bath, supplicants and petitioners surrounded him. He sat down, wrapped in a robe, and proceeded to hear their cases. His loyal servant, attending to the rabbi's personal needs, prepared a cup of water and wine and held it for him. But Rabbi Yehudah haNasi was so engrossed in the people's business that he couldn't spare the time to take the cup. The servant stood and stood until gradually he fell asleep, cup in hand. When the rabbi finally saw his servant, clutching the unused cup and sleeping, he said, "Solomon put it well: 'Sweet is the sleep of the laborer, whether he eats little or much; but the satiety of the rich will not suffer him to sleep' [Kohelet 5:11]."[6] As the Midrash observes of Rabbi Yehudah haNasi and those like him, "Those rich in Torah like ourselves are so busy attending to the needs of the people that we are not even allowed to sleep."[7]

Even mentors should be allowed to sleep. And to live! And it is the rested, nurtured mentors who will be the most reliable guides to crafting a life worth living.

Completing the Circle

Chapter Eleven

Who Heals the Healers?

Remember what originally motivated you to serve as a leader? Recall the passion, the energy, and the love that made you decide to become a mentor. Think of your love for the Jewish people and your desire to serve. Think of your urge to build a community and to place yourself near its center. Then consider, above all, your commitment to something even greater, to *k'dushah,* a sense of holiness, a sense that people and communities can rise above their limitations and somehow be more than they had been. Rambam said that the sages are *rofei han'fashot,* healers of souls. On a personal note, I will say that that is what I wanted to be when I became a rabbi. I imagine that it is what you seek, too. Whether we are private citizens, administrators, volunteers, cantors, officers, educators, or rabbis, we yearn to be able to share our soul with others and heal their souls with the wisdom of our own. As partners with our protégés, we long to bind ourselves up in a great union of beauty and profundity, of righteousness and truth. Yet sometimes along the way we stumble. We start to surrender to the challenges that assault us as leaders and mentors. We start to feel our wounds.

Among the most severe of our challenges is that our protégés expect from us nothing less than everything. Mentors are the ones who should have every answer. We are the ones who ought to provide infinite time. Leaders are the ones who ought to attend every event and every committee meeting, conduct every program, visit every class in every school, participate in every communal event. The problem here is not that those we mentor feel this entitlement. The hidden truth (I think most of us will agree) is that deep down we mentors harbor a sense that this is a reasonable expectation. We think we don't, but we often do. We may think that *they* ought to have more limited expectations of us, but the truth is that *we* keep trying to squeeze more and more into less and less. We believe that if we would only hustle a little more, be a little more available, or organize ourselves a little more efficiently, we would finally turn our community around. Our classes, programs, and buildings would overflow with passionate, engaged, observant, and learned people! If only we were working a little harder! And so we disappoint ourselves. We grow tired. We grow weary. We grow resentful.

We are pushed up against one of the greatest contradictions of our people: their profound and deep-seated ambivalence toward Judaism and Jewish institutions. We must recognize that this ambivalence is not the same as hostility. Our people are greatly attracted to the very faith and people who repel them. So long as the Torah is kept closed and under wraps, they cry when they see it. But ask our *talmidim* to open it, read from it, and live it, and we stir the other side of the ambivalence.

Our people are trapped by ambivalence. Constantly battling their contradictory tendencies can reduce a mentor to befuddled despair.

That age-old popular ambivalence toward mentors and Judaism can crush our spirit. Some of us train to be rabbis, cantors, or educators because Judaism is our love and our passion. We sing with all the passion we can muster, and our disciples tell us that liturgical music is boring. We organize a new curriculum, and they ask us to shorten the class so that they can get home to watch a game. We devote countless hours (and often make significant financial sacrifices) because of our belief in the Jewish community and Jewish peoplehood.

And each time we do, something inside us dies. That death produces a kind of loneliness that is far deeper than what we feel when we are merely sitting alone. It is the frustration of seeing a potential squandered or witnessing a cherished value eclipsed. It is the loneliness of not being understood, of not being heard. It is the challenge of meeting indifference.

I want to conclude this book by addressing the existential loneliness that can afflict leaders and mentors. I want us to ask, Who heals the healers? We who try to make time for our people—where do we retire for renewal? Where do we go to seek encouragement, comfort, and understanding? How can we revitalize ourselves so that we have the energy to continue preaching, singing, organizing, teaching, and caring? For we know that beneath their ambivalence, our *talmidim* do want us to be doing what we do. Indeed, our people need us to be doing what we do.

We know that being a mentor, in addition to its unparalleled joys and exultation, entails being hurt, so we must look with some urgency for reliable healing. *"Mei'ayin yavo ezri?"* ("from where will my help come?")[1] Where can we mentors turn for help?

The first source of our renewal and recovery has to be attentiveness to ourselves. In the seventeenth century, Rabbi Moses Zacuto saw an allusion to this truth in the biblical verse in which God tells Abraham, *"Lech-l'cha"* ("Go forth").[2] Rabbi Zacuto understood that term hyperliterally: "Look to yourself, go to yourself." He said, "Search and discover the root of your soul, so you can fulfill it and restore it to its source." If we don't take care of ourselves first, we cannot hope to care for others. If our message does not inspire us, it is not going to inspire anyone else.

But the isolated self cannot be our only source of rejuvenation. You cannot be a Jew alone. Indeed, you cannot be a person alone, and it is our very humanity that concerns us. Our second source of renewal must involve our loved ones. Let us ask ourselves: When on our deathbed, what is it we will consider a mark of a life well lived?

Will we recall only the institution made stronger by our presence? the lives we made more whole? the services or agencies we created? the Jews able to celebrate their heritage because of us? Certainly those achievements are real and beautiful. But primarily, I imagine, we will be thinking about our loved ones, of the time we spent with them.

We need to care for our loved ones, for as Rabbi Abraham Ibn Ezra commented "A person who has a family is likened to a branch attached to its source."[3] Notice that we are not the family's source: the family is *our* source. Being connected to our loved ones is what enables us to celebrate life's delights and withstand the rigors that life throws our way. So let's love the ones we love. Let's be with them and show them how precious they are to us. Let us set them among our greatest priorities.

Third, we must be able to look to our community as well for strength and renewal. When my mother-in-law died, my wife and my communities—the synagogue we attend and the wonderful people connected to the University of Judaism (my workplace)—organized our meals, set up our home for the *shiva* minyan, consoled us, entertained our children, and made their love a source of great comfort and connection. I know that we all need similar experiences of love and care offered by our communities, whether we are a mentor or a protégé.

We can embrace that love and let it lift and sustain us. But we need to know also that the love of those we mentor is mixed with a significant dose of transference and illusion. That love is not simply for us as individuals but for their image of who they think we are as their mentors. Their affection is, therefore, special and distinct. We can embrace our community of *talmidim* provided that we are careful not to confuse them with our family or our friends. There will be some that may indeed become friends, but they all can be a source of pride, love, and joy.

Fourth, beyond community, we must be sure to look to other mentors for understanding and support. We live in a strange world, one in which we talk as though we are each other's colleagues, yet we may act as though we are each other's competitors. At the same time, nobody will understand us the way another mentor can. Nobody else can know what it is like to juggle the infinite demands we have to meet, to master the range of skills we have to use, or to reinvent the array of programs we have to present every year. Nobody but another leader knows what that constant "being on" is like. If we cannot be a haven for each other, how can we expect sanctuary anywhere in the world?

Let us work together to be affectionate with each other. The Talmud teaches that the *Kadosh Baruch Hu*, the Holy Blessing One, loves when two sages gather together and learn with each other and from each other.[4] Let us be others' mentors, confidants, and friends. If we can become a true *hevruta*, fellowship, for one another, then our collegiality will provide the strength to take what we receive from each other and to pass it along to our protégés.

There are, I believe, two further sources of strength to mention. The first is the Torah itself. A Midrash teaches us, "Words of Torah are comparable to the elixir of life."[5] Rooted in Torah, we regain our energy, direction, and composure. The Torah is for us both a guide and a filter. It teaches us how to live our lives, it establishes our priorities, and it delineates what it is that we have to give each other. My rebbe, Rabbi Simon Greenberg, of blessed memory, used to greet graduates of the Jewish Theological Seminary by asking us the most painful of questions: "What *massechet* (volume of the Talmud) are you learning now?" Of course Rabbi Greenberg's intention (and often his impact) was to encourage us to persist in our efforts to study and to learn.

Mentors ought to be learning all the time not because it is a professional expectation but because it is an existential necessity. If we cut ourselves off from what our real business is, which is to be students of Torah, we will have nothing left but committee meetings and budgets (God help us!). We abandon our time for study at the peril of our authenticity, energy, and passion. On the occasion of his ninetieth birthday, Rabbi Greenberg reminded a convention of rabbis, *"Lulei*

Toratcha sha'ashu'ai az avad'ti v'anyi" (Unless the Torah had been my constant delight, I would have perished in my affliction).[6]

Aharon, aharon, haviv—the last mentioned is the most dear. Our deepest healing radiates from the Ribbono shel Olam—the Source of the Torah—the One who gave us life, who sustains us, and who is love. *Adonai Hu ha-Elohim*—the Holy One is our God.[7] We mentors need to assert control a little less and trust a little more: "Look to the rock from whence you were hewn."[8] What we have to teach the world is that God's love is something we do not earn; it is a gift freely given. Our very being is a gift given to each of us by God, and it is a gift we can shine back on God.

The prophet Jeremiah recognized that truth when he heard God saying *"V'ahavat olam ahavtich"* (I have loved you with an endless love).[9] Do we allow ourselves to feel God's infinite love? Do we let ourselves slow down long enough to relish the moment as something pure and sacred and glorious? Look around. Breathe in the world and its wonders. The God who called us into life and gave us life as a gift, the God who gave us a Torah to love and the talent to share that love with other people—that God is the river that can nourish our roots even amid the inevitable heat and bruising we will endure. And if we are too busy to feel the overwhelming reality of God's love, then I would submit we are too busy to mentor God's people. It is time to slow down and remember in whose service we glory.

The Talmud notes, *"Hacham adif minavi"* (A sage is greater than a prophet).[10] Why? Prophets weren't encumbered with contracts—we are. Prophets were never constrained by budgets—we are. Prophets did not answer to boards of directors or raise funds to build buildings —we do. Prophets did not practice time management by making lists in personal digital assistants and appointment books—but we do. It sounds to me as though the prophets were a lot better off than we mentors are. So why is a leader, a mentor, greater than a prophet?

The reason for the greatness of the mentor over that of the prophet is that mentors are the ones who have not heard the thundering voice, nor seen the lightning, nor felt the miracle firsthand. We do not possess the assuring certainty of "thus says the Holy One." Yet we are willing to bear witness to that evocative reality just behind the parochet. Without certainty, we commit our lives to the conviction that what we do matters, that all people are God's children, that God is served in acts of goodness and moments of grace. In a world where God is masked, we make our hands God's hands and allow our hearts to care on God's behalf.

The Talmud records, "Many people may be monarchs, but not many can be sages."[11] We are among those people privileged to share and propagate God's Torah, which our people so desperately need. We are the ones who are able—by the way we live our lives, by the institutions we build, by the agencies we serve, and by the way we speak to and treat each other—to testify to the beauty of our heritage, its wisdom, and its glory. Our people still need leaders to emulate. They still need their mentors.

My blessing for all of us in the journeys ahead is that we continue to provide that kind of leadership for each other, leadership that testifies to the greatness of God and the insight of our Torah, and that the fellowship we build with each other will light a flame that will illumine all the Jewish people and, through them, all the world.

My brothers and my sisters, fellow mentors, I pray that this will be for us a path of great healing, of great solace, and of great wisdom. Having gathered strength and nourishment from its source, we will then be able to share those gifts with our brothers and sisters, the House of Israel, all humankind, and all Creation.

Appendix

With Abounding Love

A Theology for the Whole Heart

> You have loved the House of Israel with an everlasting love.
> —Siddur

> You shall love THE HOLY ONE your God with all your heart.
> —Siddur

Relationship is the key to effective mentoring. Without a willingness to enter into a caring and committed relationship, it is impossible to serve as a guide or a role model for a *talmid*. But by embracing such a role, we give form to the centrality of relationship for all Jewish expression and life. At the very core of Judaism is a love relationship: between God and the Jewish people, between Jewish communities and their leaders, between the generations and Torah, between groups of seekers and their mentors. A central assumption of all Jewish spirituality is that only in a relationship can we grow to incorporate holiness into our identity.

Only in covenant can a context of sanctity and profundity emerge. Since the mentor-*talmid* relationship is a reflection and an expression of a more embracing love, that between the Jewish people and

God, the efforts to become a mentor can be strengthened only if we think through what our age-old love affair with God can mean in a modern age.

How we relate to God profoundly affects our Jewish behavior, and, equally important, how we perceive God relating to us profoundly affects our willingness to act as mentors, and our participation in building community. This appendix will articulate a model of relationship that provides grounds for building rich relationships between each other as a religious imperative. In the process of building a theology of relationship, this model will also offer a conception of *halachah* as binding yet volitional, simultaneously divine and human. It maintains the centrality of Jewish peoplehood and requires traditional commitments while insisting on the individual autonomy expected by modernity.

The Central Issue

The central issue that any Jewish theology must attempt to explicate is that of authority.[1] Whether God spoke discrete words to Moses at Sinai or the Jewish people responded to God's inspiring presence by committing to writing an inspired response[2] is an argument reduced to a dispute about method, about the means God used to communicate a message. In either case, the end product is a work that embodies God's will. An issue more fundamental than the form of Revelation is the nature of God's authority. Our perception of that authority determines how we relate to God. In other words, how does the nature of the Jewish relationship with God accommodate both God's authority and our conscience?[3]

Authority manifests two major modes: internal and external.[4] External authority is force. It neither implies nor requires consent on the part of the individual or group coerced.[5] The government provides the most obvious examples of external authority: young people are forced into conscription; civilians are forced to serve on juries and pay taxes. Such authority is overwhelmingly external and largely authoritarian. This is not to say that government is immoral, just that the ideal government is generally dispassionate about one code of morality in particular and enforces consent and obedience regardless of the citizen's individual perspective. The motivation to comply is enforced through threats and coercion. Such an authority is outside the framework of morality, since it is unconcerned with autonomous consent and generally inhibits the development of autonomy.

Ultimately, however, external authority alone is inadequate to compel behavior. Authority can produce action only with the consent of the people involved. A government can jail a protester for refusing to fight a war, but only that protester has the power to agree to fight. External authority ultimately relies on internal authority to produce a desired response. External authority is limited to negatives—it can prevent some actions; it can punish noncompliance—but compliance always results from some measure of inner commitment (whether coerced or not).

As an external authority, this limitation applies to God as well. God may be the source of ultimate authority, but Jews still perform mitzvot only if they consent to do so. People may serve God out of fear, but it is the people alone who agree to do so. Construed by some sacred literature (and in some people's minds) as an external authority, God's power—in that understanding—is merely negative: it is the power to punish noncompliance.

The second type of authority is internal—a powerful mode of authority in Jewish tradition.[6] It is the only form that can guide most contemporary Jews within the sphere of morality, since it alone is concerned with the motives and priorities of the responding individual. Only human choice can supply the internal authority—the motivation to act, the self-induced compulsion to respond.[7]

Internal authority itself can utilize a positive or a negative motivation. We can feel compelled to act out of fear (a negative motivation in that we act to avoid an undesirable consequence) or out of love (a positive motivation in that we act to gain a positive goal). But in either case, the motivation to act emerges from within.[8] Action based on fear may be related to external authority: because we wish to forestall punishment, we choose to comply. But ultimately the action springs from an internal decision: we decide whether or not to conform. Actions based on love may also be related to an external being: because a good friend asks us to volunteer, we do it despite the fact that we really don't feel like doing it. Although we are responding to an external demand, we freely choose to act; we act out of love. Our internal authority takes command.

The two modes of internal authority, fear and love, have a long history in Judaism. Both *yirat shamayim* (fear of heaven) and *ahavat haShem* (love of God) find ample attestation in traditional texts.[9] Generally, the two are complementary aspects of an individual's relationship with God. Yet inevitably individuals tend to emphasize one mode over the other.

That same tendency is true for communities as well. Certain Jewish communities, while not disavowing *ahavat haShem*, perceived *yirat shamayim* as the highest form of human piety. Particularly during the Middle Ages,[10] as exemplified in the *Tahanun* (petitionary prayers),[11] the notion of *yirat shamayim* dominated. God was all; humanity was nothing. The natural consequence of that view is to expect human-divine relating to work in one direction: God commands, and people obey. *Halachah* is treated as immutable because people, including community leaders, are overwhelmed by a sense of their inadequacy and their insignificance.

In such a schema, the model for the human relationship with God is that of servant to master, subject to monarch. Not only are the members of the relationship unequal, but the form of the relationship is also hierarchical. Rabbi Joseph Soloveitchik wrote, "Covenantal man feels overpowered and defeated by God even when he appears to be a free agent of his own will."[12] The highest form of human response becomes complete, unquestioning acquiescence.

The view that stresses *yirat shamayim* continues to be held in our day. It comes with a long Jewish history and numerous aspects that commend it. But it cannot serve as a mentor's primary model for relating to God. The needs of our community direct us to *ahavat haShem* as a model in which to ground our more humanist relationship.[13] Such an approach also finds ample support in Jewish literature. One noteworthy precedent is Maimonides. In the section of the *Mishneh Torah* on *hilchot t'shuvah* (the laws of Repentence), he discusses the two ways of relating to God and states that serving God out of fear is not "the standard set by the prophets and sages." He commends this approach as a temporary educational measure, useful to train *talmidim* to serve God out of fear "until their knowledge shall have increased when they will serve out of love."[14]

Modernity, with its insistence on the worth of the individual and the ability of humanity to progress, has moved us beyond the utility of fear as a functional training device. If Jews who wish to be modern also desire to draw close to God, they will do so out of love.

Relationship

Focusing on relationship means that we express the idea that Judaism—living Jewishly—is not an affirmation of static dogma or fixed practice. Rather, it is a willingness to participate in a relationship with God through identification with the Jewish people and through practice of the tradition. Such a model is dynamic to its core. The religion and culture of the Jewish people have taken several forms throughout the course of history. Like other relationships, the connection between the Jewish people and God has grown, changed, and developed. What makes the evolving religious expressions Judaism, what links us to our ancestors, is that we are all partners in the age-old love affair between the Jewish people and God. The Song of Songs presents a model for understanding our tie to God as relationship, building on the Talmudic reading of the text as a love lyric about God and the Jewish people. No other ancient text focuses to such a degree on the image of marriage that binds God and the people.[15] It is rooted in the prophetic tradition, in which God claims Israel as a bride.[16] This model establishes the primary relationship as between God and the entire Jewish people (as opposed to between God and Jewish individuals). God and Israel owe each other fidelity, and their vows to each other are embodied in Torah. Throughout the prophetic books, God is presented as Israel's spouse and Israel as God's bride.

The fact that there is a love relationship between the Jewish people and God does not imply that there is an equality with God. It does, however, imply that God expects, even needs, a mature relationship—one that requires the Jews to act autonomously in order for the love relationship to develop fully. Ontologically we may be inferior to God, but Israel is nonetheless God's partner and therefore must act as an equal in the relationship in order for the love to be fully developed.

This model of a relationship between God and the Jewish people bears clear implications for the relationship between a mentor and a protégé. Although the partners are not necessarily equals in experience, knowledge, or insight, their relationship is nonetheless one of mutuality, caring, and commitment. A covenant exists between mentor and *talmidim*, and it manifests itself, as does the Jewish relationship with God, through deeds (*mitzvot*), through loyalty, and through love.

Mitzvot

The model of a love relationship also provides us with a way of understanding mitzvot as the expression of the way in which God and the Jewish people relate to each other: while retaining the sense of divine authority, the Jewish people recognize the dynamic, interactional nature of mitzvot. A healthy relationship requires that both partners try to meet each other's needs, that both adopt to each other's concerns as their own. Mitzvot are the ground on which those accommodations take place, where Israel meets God's needs (by translating love into sacred deeds) and God meets Israel's (by offering a way of life that is profound, beautiful, and holy). It is an error to speak of mitzvot as solely God-given. It is equally fallacious to consider them purely the projection of human needs. The only realistic notion of mitzvot is that they are developed between God and Israel: they are the give-and-take of our relationship, a symbol of love between the two lovers.

Mitzvot are the logical implication that God is a real presence and that we have a relationship with God. Were there no Deity, anything would be permitted. Were our relationship with God solely that of Sovereign Eternal One and abject subject, we would do nothing we desired. But the loving relationship is demonstrated in action, by the meeting of needs: "You have affirmed this day that the Holy One is your God and that you will walk in God's ways."[17] In the same way, the authority of a mentor might appear to rely on externals: position, title, income, status. But the real catalyst for inner growth and community building is internal: the love and loyalty that the relationship can inspire.

God's authority is experienced as internal (despite sacred literature that can be read otherwise): it arises from our desire to maintain and deepen our relationship with God, our lover. God requests the mitzvot as a need; we perform the mitzvot because we are committed to the relationship, because our lover has a need. That need is itself sufficient to impel our performance. The mitzvot do not have to be rational (often they are not). From the human perspective, they have merely to be a need of God's, and we are under the same kind of obligation to perform them that we are under when a friend, a lover, or a spouse makes a request or articulates a need. If we are to continue the relationship, we must accept the action as obligatory. It is in this sense that the mitzvot are binding. This is what we mean by *kabbalat ol malchut shamayim* (accepting the yoke of the sovereignty of heaven), which is, after all, a choice. God, in turn, takes on the obligation of a committed relationship with the House of Israel: "I shall be your God and you shall be my people."[18] The *hovah* (obligation), like all moral authorities, must be internal; it must spring from love—for us and for God. There is no other way to be obligated in our age.

And just as with any other love relationship, we retain the option to deny the need. We can choose not to perform the mitzvah, but only at the cost of harming the relationship. I can choose not to fulfill my wife's need, but our marriage will suffer. Not performing a mitzvah is the same act, and the relationship between God and the Jewish people bears the consequence. Love not renewed grows stale.

From God's perspective, then, the mitzvot are also obligatory, since they also represent for God the maintenance of a relationship with the Jews, who wish to be God's lovers. Our willingness to live in Covenant binds God, since God must accord our actions divine status. Examples of the way in which Jewish ritual forces God's hand are easy to elucidate: weddings performed according to *halachah* change the metaphysical status of the people involved. A *brit milah* (circumcision) and a bar or bat mitzvah celebration—acts performed by and among people—are ratified by God. Judaism teaches that God responds to human initiative; God accords status to our rulings. We must meet divine needs, and God must meet ours: "A person acts alone, and God blesses all the work of his hands."[19] That, too, is a consequence of our mutual relationship.

An example of this notion is found in the Mishnah: "Rainwater that falls from a tree naturally is not susceptible for transmitting impurity. If the water is shaken off deliberately, however, it is susceptible."[20] God changes the metaphysical status of the water based solely on human intervention. God ratifies the human decision.

God meets human needs. The mitzvot are the way in which God and *am Yisrael*, the nation of Israel, relate to each other. Love, to stay alive, must translate into action; that action is embodied in the mitzvot.[21]

God is Israel's spouse. The two are partners in a passionate love affair. That love provides its own eternal justification. The relationship means that both partners must bend their will toward that of the other. Both must address the needs of the other. The love of our relationship is enacted through mitzvot, a human-divine process of meeting the other's needs and expressing our love for each other.

God and Individual Jews

God's primary connection has traditionally been understood to pertain to the Jewish people as an entity. But there must also be room for individuals to form a personal relationship with God. A person is the product of both environment and heredity, which contribute to the formation of the personality that is unique to each soul.[22] In other words, people are who they are in part because of both character and culture. For "culture" we can substitute "tradition," and for "character" we can substitute "conscience." We relate to God through those two poles, through tradition and conscience, both as members of the Jewish people and as individuals.

No relationship has only one strand. Parents relate to their children as mentors, teachers, friends, and parents. Those elements add strength, complexity, and depth to the relationship. So, too, do we relate to God in several ways, as members of a community and as individuals, thus adding to the totality of the relationship.[23] The prophet Hosea pointed to a way of placing that framework into our relationship model by viewing God as husband, Israel as wife, and individual Jew as child.[24] This schema implies that as individuals we do not share the same claim of partnership and equality with God that we claim as members of *am Yisrael*. As individuals, we relate to God as parents, teachers, even friends. The bond is strong and personal, but it is still secondary to our attachment as members of a larger community. The mature relationship is expressed through the larger Jewish community. For that reason, *halachic* changes, changes in relating, are primarily effected through the community; they are influenced, but not determined, by individual, private choice.

Contemporary Jewish movements are best understood within this rubric as collections of individuals. Each collection bands together to reflect its common understanding of its relationship with God (or the cosmos or nature or however the group perceives ultimate reality). We can understand the individual denominations within Judaism as collections of like-minded individuals. They band together with others like themselves to express their relationship to God, but it is only the totality, *am Yisrael,* that has the status of a spouse. Movements come and go; the Jewish people are eternal.

And remember: just as we have several loving relationships simultaneously, so does God relate with love to different groups of people—all at the same time. No group shares the same relationship with God. And no group should have to meet the same requirements as another group. There is room for different Jewish groups, just as there is room for non-Jewish groups.

This notion of multiple relationships, each one distinct, is crucial to transforming the debate (and animosity) within Judaism.[25] By recognizing that God can have more than one relationship, that not all denominations or coalitions need to address the same demands, we shift the focus of the Jewish polemic. Without surrendering the subjective preference for one or the other, we can henceforth dispense with terms like illegitimate and inauthentic. It is no more reasonable to call Orthodox Judaism inflexible than it is to call a father inflexible because he doesn't fulfill one's expectations of a business partner. There are different needs and expectations in different relationships. Just as a friend is not inauthentic for not relating as a spouse, so Reform Judaism is not inauthentic for not relating to God as more traditional practice would dictate. Relationships vary with varying participants. So long as those relationships meet certain minimal standards of love and support and continuity, they attain the level of Jewish legitimacy.[26]

But authenticity is not the same as closeness. Each movement (or coalition within a movement) retains different ways of relating to God. It is still valuable for each to critique and dissent from other forms of Jewish expression, recognizing that its comments emerge from its particular perception of Judaism and God. Ultimately, however, it is the Jewish totality, *klal Yisrael*, with whom God maintains *kiddushin* (marriage). As individuals, the offspring of that marriage, we participate according to our understanding of the demands of that relationship. It is only with the entire people, however, that the relationship is consummated.[27]

Implications

This theological model provides three general advantages: it establishes a positive value for joining the community (why be Jewish?), it sets up a way to express that relationship (how can one be Jewish?), and it legitimizes diverse approaches to Judaism without compromising the integrity of any particular version of Judaism or abandoning Jewish unity. Different denominations and individual Jews understand the contours of their love relationship with God differently. Yet all see themselves as part of that larger Covenant. Recognizing the centrality of relationship in Judaism proves that Judaism must produce mentors; if it does not, the religion contradicts one of its primary tenets.

Today, now, God makes the same demand of us that God made of our ancestors: Love me. Live in *kiddushin* with me. Be Jewish—live the mitzvot as your community understands what that commitment entails. Live in a Jewish context so that you can participate in a time-tested and intimate love affair with me as a full partner in our relationship.

Viewed through the prism of the model of relationship, *halachah* and all of Jewish tradition are expressions of the Jewish Covenant with God. Just as relationships retain the form of past interactions but must change to reflect the experiences the lovers have gone through together, so *halachah*, as the dynamic system in which Jews and God cultivate their relationship, must reflect both where the Jewish people have been and what our current needs are. The ideal of relationship argues against both abandoning *halachah* and freezing it. Instead, relationship teaches that God and *am Yisrael* have a perpetual partnership in the formation and revamping of *halachah*.

Finally, looking at our tie with God as a love relationship allows us to appreciate other forms of Jewish and religious expression without delegitimizing the integrity of any denomination. As individuals, we continue to claim centrality for our own understanding of Judaism. We also recognize, however, the theological backdrop against which to appreciate the unity (as opposed to the uniformity) of the entire House of Israel.

This book began by noting the dangerous dichotomy between wisdom and knowledge and calling for a return to a Jewish path of wholeness, holiness, and connection. If God is known through relationship, if membership in the Jewish people is an expression of the relationship, and if Jewish living is a celebration of that relationship, then God, the Jewish people, and Judaism can be fostered only in the context of relationship. By summoning the courage to stand as someone's role model, counselor, and guide—by becoming someone's mentor—we make such a relationship possible. Embodying the commitment, love, and hope that can be established only one person at a time, a mentor gives God's love shape and texture. In the act of caring and guiding, the mentor reveals the One who cares and guides us all.

The mentor is nothing less than the beacon through which God's light shines into our lives.

We all could use a little more light.

We all could use a mentor.

And we all can become one.

Reading Lists for Mentors (and Mentors-to-Be)

The selections listed below do not include the sacred classics of the Jewish religion (the Torah, the Talmud, and so on). My assumption is that leaders and mentors (and mentors-in-training) will have had ample opportunity to acquire a Jewish education. For an extensive bibliography of Jewish writings, see "Talmud Torah," chapter 12 of my book *It's a Mitzvah! Step-by-Step to Jewish Living* (West Orange, N.J., and New York: Behrman House and Rabbinical Assembly, 1995).

Adler, Mortimer J. **How to Speak, How to Listen**. New York: Touchstone, 1983.

Bok, Sissela. **Lying: Moral Choice in Public and Private Life**. New York: Vintage, 1989.

Borowitz, Eugene B. "The Ideal Jew." In **Exploring Jewish Ethics: Papers on Covenant Responsibility**, 226–37. Detroit: Wayne State University Press, 1990.

Daloz, Laurent A. Parks, Cheryl H. Keen, James P. Keen, and Sharon Daloz Parks. **Common Fire: Leading Lives of Commitment in a Complex World.** Boston: Beacon Press, 1996.

Friedman, Edwin H. **Generation to Generation: Family Process in Church and Synagogue**. New York: Guilford Press, 1985.

————. **Friedman's Fables**. New York: Guilford Press, 1990.

Gilligan, Carol. **In a Different Voice: Psychological Theory and Women's Development**. Cambridge, Mass.: Harvard University Press, 1982.

Green, Arthur. "**The Zaddik as Axis Mundi in Later Judaism**." *Journal of American Academy of Religion* 45, no. 3 (1977): 327–47. Reprinted in *Essential Papers in Kabbalah*, 291–314, edited by Lawrence Fine. New York: New York University Press, 1995.

Heifetz, Ronald. **Leadership Without Easy Answers**. Cambridge, Mass.: Belknap Press, 1998.

Jones, James W. **Contemporary Psychoanalysis and Religion: Transference and Transcendence**. New Haven, Conn.: Yale University Press, 1991.

Kotter, John P. **On What Leaders Really Do**. Cambridge, Mass.: Harvard Business School Press, 1999.

Telushkin, Joseph. **Words That Hurt, Words That Heal: How to Choose Words Wisely and Well**. New York: William Morrow, 1996.

Weisberg, Jacob. **Does Anybody Listen? Does Anybody Care?** Englewood, Colo.: Medical Group Management Association, 1994.

Wildavsky, Aaron. **The Nursing Father: Moses as a Political Leader**. Tuscaloosa: University of Alabama Press, 1984.

Notes

Preface

1. Elisabeth Kübler-Ross, *On Life After Death* (Berkeley, Calif.: Celestial Arts, 1991), 25–26.

2. Exodus 35:31.

3. Bava Metzia 33a.

An Invitation

1. Genesis 23:1. For further discussion, see Bradley Shavit Artson, *The Bedside Torah: Wisdom, Visions, and Dreams* (McGraw-Hill, 2001).

2. Genesis 22:20–23.

3. Kohelet 1:5.

4. For a discussion of the rationale for translating *Baruch* as Blessing rather than as the more conventional Blessed, see "Barukh ha-Shem: God Is Bountiful," *Conservative Judaism*, Winter 1994, reprinted in Vicki Kelman, *Family Room: Linking Families into a Jewish Learning Community* (Los Angeles: Shirley and Arthur Whizin Institute for Jewish Family Life, 1995).

5. B'reishit Rabbah 58:2.

Chapter One

1. The Hebrew word *rabbi* means "my teacher; my master."

2. Indeed, so great was this association of Torah with a mentor that when Rabbi Eliezer fell ill, his students justified their fear and grief by crying, "Is it possible that a Torah Scroll dwells in pain and we do not weep?" (Sanhedrin 101a).

3. Derech Eretz Zuta 5.

4. Cited by Gregg Easterbrook, "Science Sees the Light: The Rediscovery of Higher Meaning," *New Republic*, October 12, 1998, 29.

5. James W. Jones, *In the Middle of This Road We Call Our Life: The Courage to Search for Something More* (San Francisco: HarperSanFrancisco, 1995), 75.

6. Alan Shapiro, *The Last Happy Occasion* (Chicago: University of Chicago Press 1996), 3.

7. Cited by Easterbrook, "Science Sees the Light," 29.

8. See David Shatz, "The Overexamined Life Is Not Worth Living," in *God and the Philosophers: The Reconciliation of Faith and Reason*, ed. Thomas V. Morris (New York: Oxford University Press, 1994), 263–85.

9. Samson Raphael Hirsch, *Collected Writings of Samson Raphael Hirsch* (New York: Feldheim, 1997), 8:319.

Chapter Two

1. There are several thinkers, often adept in both science and theology, who are working through ways of seeing from these broader vistas. Three worthy trailblazers and their works are John Polkinghorne, *Belief in God in an Age of Science* (New Haven, Conn.: Yale University Press, 1998), John Hick, *An Interpretation of Religion: Human Responses to the Transcendent* (New Haven, Conn.: Yale University Press, 1989), and Arthur Peacocke, *Paths from Science Towards God: The End of All Our Exploring* (Oxford: Oneworld, 2001).

2. For an extensive discussion of this point with a wise application to religion, see James W. Jones, *Contemporary Psychoanalysis and Religion: Transference and Transcendence* (New Haven, Conn.: Yale University Press, 1991).

3. An insightful introduction to this "relational" way of reading can be found in Peter Ochs, ed., *The Return to Scripture in Judaism and Christianity: Essays in Postcritical Scriptural Interpretation* (Mahwah, N.J.: Paulist Press, 1993). See also Robert Scholes, *Protocols of Reading* (New Haven, Conn.: Yale University Press, 1989).

4. For a fine analysis of this development, see Jack Wertheimer, *A People Divided: Judaism in Contemporary America* (New York: Basic Books, 1993); for denominational applications, see Neil Gillman, *Conservative Judaism: The New Century* (West Orange, N.J.: Behrman House, 1993), Daniel J. Elazar and Rela Mintz Geffen, *The Conservative Movement in Judaism* (Albany: State University of New York Press, 2000), Jack Wertheimer, *Jews in the Center: Conservative Synagogues and Their Members* (New Brunswick, N.J.: Rutgers University Press, 2000), and Michael Meyer, *Response to Modernity: A History of the Reform Movement in Judaism* (New York: Oxford University Press, 1988), ch. 10.

5. Jeffrey H. Tigay, *Deuteronomy: The Traditional Hebrew Text with the New JPS Translation/Commentary* (Philadelphia: Jewish Publication Society, 1996), 5.

6. For a magisterial discussion of Torah as Judaism and its application by a foremost scholar of Jewish studies, see Jacob Neusner, *Torah Through the Ages: A Short History of Judaism* (London: SCM Press, 1990).

7. Ketubot 67b. Many of the *aggadot* (rabbinic legends and tales) and *midrashim* (rabbinic narratives and interpretations) found in this chapter are from *Judah Nadich, The Legends of the Rabbis* (Northvale, N.J.: Jason Aronson, 1994).

8. Horayot 10a–b; Berachot 28a.

9. Eugene B. Borowitz, "The Ideal Jew," in *Exploring Jewish Ethics: Papers on Covenant Responsibility* (Detroit: Wayne State University Press, 1990), 227.

10. Sofrim 16:6, 41b.

11. Josephus, Antiquities 12:2.5, 12.4.1.

12. Deuteronomy 34:10.

13. Exodus 2:17. In addition to the biblical and rabbinic portrayals and explorations of his character, Moses has inspired many fine recent works spanning a range of fields. In poetry, see Anthony Burgess, *Moses: A Narrative* (New York: Stonehill, 1976). In fiction, see Sholem Asch, *Moses* (New York: G. P. Putnam's Sons, 1951), and Thomas Mann, *The Tables of the Law* (New York: Alfred A. Knopf, 1964). In biblical studies, see James Nohrnberg, *Like unto Moses: The Constituting of an Interruption* (Bloomington: Indiana University Press, 1995). In political science, see Aaron Wildavsky, *The Nursing Father: Moses as a Political Leader* (Tuscaloosa: University of Alabama Press, 1984). In philosophy, see Martin Buber, *Moses: The Revelation and the Covenant* (Atlantic Highlands, N.J.: Humanities Press International, 1946). A wonderful book that transcends categorization is Jonathan Hirsch, *Moses: A Life* (New York: Ballantine Books, 1998).

14. Sh'mot Rabbah 1:32.

15. Cited in Menachem M. Kasher, *The Passover Haggadah* (New York: Shengold, 1964), 246.

16. Sh'mot Rabbah 2:2.

17. Sh'mot Rabbah 2:11.

18. Numbers 11:12.

19. Sifrei Beha'alotcha 91.

20. Numbers 11:11.

21. Numbers 11:17.

22. Numbers 11:24-25.

23. Numbers 11:29.

24. It remains one of the ironies of Jewish life that at virtually every Passover Seder the leader draws the participants' attention to the omission of Moses's name and then praises his humility and character at great length. Many *haggadot* now print a comment about this omission as a note to be read during the service! For a fine and nuanced paean to Moses, see Walter Kaufmann, "The Old Testament," in *The Faith of a Heretic* (New York: New American Library, 1978), 171–206.

25. Exodus 32:7.

26. B'rachot 32a.

27. Mechilta de–Mentor Shimon bar Yohai 1:1–6:2.

28. Sh'mot Rabbah 5:22. These and other legends about Moses can be found in Aaron Routhkoff, "Moses, in the Aggadah," in *Encyclopaedia Judaica* (New York: Macmillan, 1971–72); 12:395–98. Two other useful compilations are Hayim Nahman Bialik and Yehoshua Hana Ravnitzky, eds., *The Book of Legends* (New York: Schocken Press, 1994), and Louis Ginzberg, *The Legends of the Jews* (Philadelphia: Jewish Publication Society, 1909–38).

29. Avot de–Mentor Natan 14:1; Sukkah 28a; Ta'anit 20b; Berachot 26a.

30. Vayikra Rabbah 35:7.

31. Deuteronomy 4:39.

32. Cited in Itturei Torah (Tel Aviv: Yavneh Publishing House, 1998), 3:196.

33. Berachot 17a.

34. Megillah 27b–28a.

35. Shabbat 31a.

36. Berachot 62a.

37. Sukkah 28a.

38. Deuteronomy 6:7.

39. Sifrei D'varim 34.

Chapter Three

1. Sukkah 56b.

2. Proverbs 1:7.

3. See John Holt, "What Parents Can Do," in *Learning All the Time* (Reading, Mass.: Addison-Wesley, 1989).

4. Niddah 30b; Seder Yetzirat haV'lad, Beit haMidrash 1:153–55.

5. This phrase, "transcending the text," comes from a fabulous study of the way in which prayer and liturgy are far more than what's on the printed page: Lawrence Hoffman, *Beyond the Text: A Holistic Approach to Liturgy* (Bloomington and Indianapolis: Indiana University Press, 1989).

6. Proverbs 22:6.

7. This is the teaching of Rabbi Eliezer (Yevamot 62b).

8. Malachi 3:24

9. Midrash Tehillim 93:13.

10. Yerushalmi Shabbat 1:1, 3a.

11. Psalm 128:3.

12. David Blumenthal, *Facing the Abusing God: A Theology of Protest* (Louisville: Westminster/John Knox Press, 1993), 77.

13. Rabbi Isaac Luria was the creative genius in sixteenth-century Tzfat, Israel, who developed the most popular form of kabbalah. See Lawrence Fine, *Physician of the Soul, Healer of the Cosmos: Isaac Luria and His Kabbalistic Fellowship* (Berkeley and Los Angeles: University of California Press, 2003).

14. Rabbi Isaiah Horowitz, *Sh'nei Luhot haBrit.*

15. Maimonides, *The Guide of the Perplexed*, trans. Shlomo Pines (Chicago: University of Chicago Press, 1963), 1:8.

16. Maimonides, *Guide of the Perplexed*, 1:71.

17. Rabbi Menachem Mendl, the Kotzker mentor, ad loc.

18. Exodus 20:12.

19. Kiddushin 30b.

20. For a comprehensive review of the *halachic* writings on this topic, see Gerald Blidstein, *Honor Thy Father and Mother: Filial Responsibility in Jewish Law and Ethics* (New York: Ktav, 1975).

21. Abraham Joshua Heschel, *The Insecurity of Freedom* (New York: Farrar, Straus and Giroux, 1966), 39–40.

22. Sefer Hasidim 13c, no. 954.

23. B'reishit Rabbah 20.

24. Mechilta de-Vayissa 7.

25. Makot 10a; Ta'anit 7a.

26. Sifrei D'varim, piska 34.

27. Danny Abse, cited in *On the Doorposts of Your House: Prayers and Ceremonies for the Jewish Home* (New York: Central Conference of American Rabbis, 1994), 311–12.

Chapter Four

1. Ketubot 111a.

2. Proverbs 31:10.

3. Midrash Mishlei 31.

4. Salomon Buber, ed., *Lekah Tov, B'reishit* (Jerusalem: Monazon, 1960 [reprint]), 23.

5. Leviticus 19:17–18.

6. B'rachot 10a.

7. Genesis 25:21.

8. B'reishit Rabbah, Toldot, 63:5.

9. Did the wife know that she was echoing the poignant words of the biblical Elkanah to his wife Hannah: "Why are you so sad? Am I not more devoted to you than ten sons?" (1 Samuel 1:8). For a discussion of issues of infertility, see Bradley Shavit Artson, "The Work of Our Hands: Infertility and Family Issues Facing the Jewish Community," *Tikkun*, May/June 2001.

10. Salomon Buber, ed., *Pesikta de Rav Kahana*, 180a.

11. B'rachot 7b.

12. Yoma 35b.

13. Vayikra Rabbah 34:3.

14. Ta'anit 7a. The saying is that of Rabba bar Bar Hanah.

15. Because of the importance of the relationship between employer and employee, Judaism offers extensive guidance on the obligations of each participant in the relationship. For a useful presentation of some of that wisdom, see Meir Tamari,

"With All Your Possessions": Jewish Ethics and Economic Life (New York: Free Press, 1987), especially ch. 6.

16. Menahot 110b.
17. B'rachot 5b.
18. Ta'anit 24a.

Chapter Five

1. Martin Buber, "Teaching and Deed," *Israel and the World: Essays in a Time of Crisis* (Syracuse, N.Y.: Syracuse University Press, 1997), 145.
2. Maimonides, Sh'monah Perakim, ch. 4.
3. Hayyim Luzzatto, Mesillat Yesharim, trans. Mordecai Kaplan (Philadelphia: Jewish Publication Society, 1936), 3.
4. For an extensive discussion of this contextualized self, see Eugene B. Borowitz, *Renewing the Covenant* (Philadelphia: Jewish Publication Society, 1991).
5. Illustrative of Moses's not having all the answers is the wonderful midrash in which he sits at the back of the school of Rabbi Akiva (some thirteen hundred years after the events of the Exodus) and can't understand Rabbi Akiva's subtle and profound readings of the Torah. When a student asks Rabbi Akiva where those teachings come from, the rabbi responds that they are *halachah l'Moshe miSinai* (law deriving from Moses at Sinai). The response of Moses is to marvel and weep (Menahot 29b).
6. Leviticus 21:17.
7. Leviticus 21:23.
8. Deuteronomy 32:5.
9. Sifrei D'varim, piska 308.
10. Deuteronomy 6:5.
11. Sanhedrin 106b.
12. Massekehet Sukkah 53a.

Chapter Six

1. Megillah 16b.
2. Pesikta Rabbati, piska 21.
3. Several honest and spiritual responses to the familial chaos of Genesis are now available, none better than Peter Pitzele, *Our Fathers' Wells: A Personal Encounter with the Myths of Genesis* (San Francisco: HarperSanFrancisco, 1995), Burton L. Vizotsky, *The Genesis of Ethics* (New York: Crown, 1996), Norman Cohen, *Self, Struggle, and Change* (Woodstock, Vt.: Jewish Lights, 1995), and Norma Rosen, *Biblical Women Unbound: Counter-Tales* (Philadelphia: Jewish Publication Society, 1996).
4. M. S. Kleinman, *Or Yesharim* (Piotrkov, 1924), 46. Cited in *The Hasidic Anthology*, trans. Louis I. Newman (Schocken Books, New York, 1963).

5. Deuteronomy 6:18.

6. Ta'anit 7a.

7. Yoma 86a.

8. Shulhan Aruch, Yoreh De'ah 246:8. Notice that reform is open even for a scholar. T'shuvah is possible for Jews of every walk of life, scholars and sages no less than any others.

9. Tanhuma B, Yitro 17; Yalkut Shimoni 286.

10. Tanhuma B, Yitro 17; Yalkut Shimoni 286.

11. B'rachot 17a.

12. Mechilta, Messechta d'Pischa 3.

13. Avot de–Mentor Natan A, 1.

14. Yerushalmi Sanhedrin 28a.

15. Of course the kicker was the fourth child to respond. He announced, "Last year I was free, but this year, I'm four!"

16. Ta'anit 4a. The quotation is from Ravina.

17. Shabbat 30b–31a.

18. P'sahim 112a.

19. Temple Grandin, *Thinking in Pictures: And Other Reports from My Life with Autism* (New York: Doubleday, 1995).

20. Avot de–Mentor Natan A, 3.

21. Mishnah Avot 5:24. Ben Bag-Bag is the quotation's source.

22. Chaim Bloch, *Gemeinde der Chassidim* (Vienna, 1920).

23. For more on the mitzvah of talmud Torah, see Bradley Shavit Artson, *It's a Mitzvah! Step-by-Step to Jewish Living* (West Orange, N.J., and New York: Behrman House and Rabbinical Assembly, 1995), ch. 14.

24. Nedarim 62a.

25. Mishnah Avot 6:6.

Chapter Seven

1. Tikunei Zohar, 70, 177b.

2. Exodus 24:12. I thank my friend and colleague Rabbi Elie Spitz for bringing this story and its interpretation to my attention.

3. Rabbi Menachem Mendl of Kotzk, cited in the *Itturei Torah, Exodus 24:12* (Tel Aviv: Yavneh Publishing House, 1998).

4. Mishnah Avot 4:1.

5. Zohar 2, 68b; Tosefta.

6. Numbers 16:4.

7. Ibn Ezra, Sefer haMivhar, Numbers 16:4. See also the comments of Rabbi Sa'adia Gaon, Rabbi Shmuel ben Meir, and Moses ben Nahman (Ramban). According to Rabbi Jacob Milgrom, this view reflects the *p'shat* (the contextual meaning of the biblical verse). See *The JPS Torah Commentary: Numbers*, commentary by Jacob Milgrom (Philadelphia: Jewish Publication Society, 1990), 131.

8. Numbers 16:5.

9. Tikunei Zohar 70, 173a.

10. This section is based directly on the superb work of Jacob Weisberg, president of Creative Communications, my former congregant, and one of my mentors. His book, *Does Anybody Listen? Does Anybody Care?* (Englewood, Colo.: Medical Group Management Association, 1994), is lucid, passionate, and masterly. His wisdom and compassion are as apparent in his life and character as in his writing. See also the wonderful book *How to Speak, How to Listen* by Mortimer J. Adler (New York: Touchstone, 1983).

11. Avodah Zarah 35a.

12. Sifrei, Beha'alotcha.

13. Pesikta Zutarta, Vayikra.

14. Beitzah 20b.

15. Zevahim 115b.

16. The source of this expression is a mystery. It is attributed to Ibn Ezra in Joseph Baron, ed., *A Treasury of Jewish Quotations* (New York: Crown, 1956), 172, who in turn cites Shirat Yisrael, 1929, 156. There, however, Ibn Ezra quotes it as an Arabic proverb. Aaron Hyman, in his encyclopedic *Otzar Divrei Hakhamim U'Fitgameihem* (Tel Aviv: Dvir, 1955), points out (correctly) that it is not found anywhere in the Talmud but that it is a popular expression that may be based on a related thought in B'rachot 6b. My thanks to Rabbis Gil Kollin, David Golinkin, and Marvin Labinger, who found these citations, and to all my Ravnet colleagues who pitched in.

17. Jeremiah 9:7.

18. Midrash Sohar Tov, Tehillim 58.

19. The most important compilation is the Hebrew work *Sefer Hafetz Hayim* by Rabbi Israel Meir Kagan. This book is so significant that the author is known by its title, Hafetz Hayim. It was first summarized in English by Rabbi Zelig Pliskin in *Guard Your Tongue* (Union City, N.J.: Gross Brothers, 1975) and by Rabbi Hillel Danziger in *The Sanctity of Speech* (Union City, N.J.: Gross Brothers, 1986). A masterly presentation of the subject in a contemporary and sensitive presentation, is Rabbi Joseph Telushkin, *Words That Hurt, Words That Heal: How to Choose Words Wisely and Well* (New York: William Morrow, 1996). For a concise discussion, see Bradley Shavit Artson, "Sh'mirat ha-Lashon: Guarding Your Tongue," in *It's a Mitzvah! Step-by-Step to Jewish Living* (West Orange, N.J., and New York: Behrman House and Rabbinical Assembly, 1995), 148–57.

20. Psalm 34:13–14.

21. Bava Batra 165a.

22. P'sahim 98b.

23. Leviticus 19:17.

24. B'reishit Rabbah 54:3.

25. Sefer Ha-Hinuch 239.

26. Cited in Joseph Telushkin, *The Book of Jewish Values: A Day-by-Day Guide to Ethical Living* (New York: Bell Tower, 2000), 2.

27. Sifrei D'varim, piska 1.

28. Proverbs 9:8.

29. Yevamot 65b.

30. Maimonides, *Mishneh Torah*, Hilchot De'ot 6:7.

31. Quoted in Telushkin, *Words That Hurt, Words That Heal*, 98.

32. Psalm 65:2.

33. Megillah 18a.

34. Megillah 18a.

35. Midrash Mishlei, ch. 26

36. Ta'anit 4a.

Chapter Eight

1. Sanhedrin 98a.

2. For more information on Jewish views of the Messiah and the messianic age, see Louis Jacobs, "The Personal Messiah—Toward the Restoration of a Discarded Doctrine," in *Principles of the Jewish Faith* (New York: Basic Books, 1964), ch. 13; Steven Schwarzschild, *The Pursuit of the Ideal: Jewish Writings of Steven Schwarzschild*, ed. Menachem Kellner (Albany: State University of New York Press, 1990); and Bradley Shavit Artson, "Triumph By Stillness and Quiet: Toward a Jewish Heroic Ideal," in *Love Peace and Pursue Peace: A Jewish Response to War and Nuclear Annihilation* (New York: United Synagogue of America, 1988).

Chapter Nine

1. Solomon Schechter, "Rabbi as Personal Example," in *Seminary Addresses and Other Papers* (New York: Burning Bush Press, 1959), 129.

2. How ironic that the self-sacrificing mentor is one contemporary adumbration of the philosopher-king in Plato's *Republic*. In Plato's dreary utopia, the philosopher-king never marries and doesn't raise his own children, both of which activities are lumped under the rubric of material distractions.

3. Solomon Schechter, "Humility and Self-Sacrifice as the Qualifications of the Rabbi," in *Seminary Addresses*, 221.

4. Schechter, "Humility and Self-Sacrifice as the Qualifications of the Rabbi," 221.

5. Pirkei de–Mentor Eliezer 42.

6. For an unsurpassed discussion of balance in life, the *derech ha-beinoni*, see Maimonides, "The Seven Chapters," in *The Maimonides Reader*, ed. Isadore Twersky (West Orange, N.J.: Behrman House), 1972.

7. D'varim Rabbah 2

8. Sefer Hasidim, no. 225. It may not be that the good leader leaves. Perhaps he or she simply becomes embittered and resentful as a result of constantly having to satisfy needs, complete tasks, and meet expectations. Maybe the community itself transforms the good leader into the bad leader! This doesn't contradict my claim that it is the mentor's responsibility to establish reasonable boundaries; it merely details the consequence of failure on that score.

9. Leviticus 19:18

10. Avot de–Mentor Natan A, 29.

11. Mishnah Avot 6:8.

12. The Youth Leadership Cabinet is a wonderful program through which local chapters of the Jewish Federation reach out to young leaders and bring them into the Federation/United Jewish Appeal system. It sponsors year-round local activities, an annual retreat, and a biennial conference in Washington, D.C., that thousands of young adults attend.

13. The Wexner Heritage Foundation runs a scholarship training program for Jewish professionals and a leadership-development program for selected adult leaders throughout North America.

14. Song of Songs 6:11.

15. Shir Hashirim Rabbah 6:11.

16. Ronald Heifetz, *Leadership Without Easy Answers* (Cambridge, Mass.: Belknap Press, 1998), 253.

17. Setting aside time is one of the principles underlying the structure of Judaism as well. Experiencing God's will as mitzvot means living with our highest standards as rules. And human beings seem built in such a way that good advice is often ignored while rules clearly articulated are easier to translate into habit. Think about how often we start a diet, then slip, abandon the effort, and start again. In contrast, most people who resolve to keep kosher are able to maintain that obligation indefinitely (even while messing up on their commitment to diet). Rules are tools to help people do what they aspire to do. See Elliot Dorff, *Mitzvah Means Commandment* (New York: United Synagogue Youth, 1989).

18. A. M. Freedman, H. I. Kaplan, and B. J. Sadock, *Comprehensive Textbook of Psychiatry*, 2nd ed. (Baltimore: Williams and Wilkins, 1975), 2:2608.

Chapter Ten

1. This is also the case with transference and countertransference. See chapter 9, note 18.

2. Sh'mot Rabbah 27:9.

3. Abraham Joshua Heschel, *The Earth Is the Lord's: The Inner World of the Jew in East Europe* (New York: Henry Schuman, 1950), 71.

4. Genesis 13:2–6.

5. Genesis 13:8–9.

6. Kohelet Rabbah 5:11, section 1.

7. Kohelet Rabbah 5:11, section 1.

Chapter Eleven

1. Psalm 121:1.

2. Genesis 12:1.

3. Rabbi Abraham ibn Ezra to Genesis 15:13.

4. Shabbat 63a.

5. Sifrei D'varim, Sifra, piska 87.

6. Psalm 119:92. This is but one of many verses in the book of Psalms that I will always associate with my rebbe, Rabbi Simon Greenberg.

7. 1 Kings 18:39.

8. Isaiah 51:1.

9. Jeremiah 31:3.

10. Bava Batra 12a.

11. Mo'ed Katan.

Appendix

1. Issues of authority are apparent in the opening of Sa'adia Gaon's *Book of Beliefs and Opinions* and in the introduction to Maimonides' *Mishneh Torah*. They permeate the thought of such recent thinkers as Franz Rosenzweig, Martin Buber, Abraham Joshua Heschel, Emanuel Levinas, Eugene Borowitz, Judith Plaskow, Irving "Yitz" Greenberg, Rebecca Alpert, Neil Gillman, Jacob Agus, Arthur Green, and Elliot Dorff.

2. For an example of the former explanation, see the response of Norman Lamm in *The Condition of Jewish Belief* (Northvale, N.J.: Jason Aronsons, 1989), 123–31. For an example of the latter, see the response of David Lieber, 140–46.

3. In more traditional categories, how do we reconcile the inherent tension between *matan Torah* and *kabbalat Torah*? See Elliot Dorff, "Revelation," *Conservative Ju-*

daism 31, no. 1–2 (1976–77): 58–59; Bradley Shavit Artson, "Thinking About Revelation," *Women's League Outlook*, Winter 1996; and Edward Greenstein, *Understanding the Sinai Revelation* (New York: Melton Research Center for Jewish Education, n.d.). For a discussion of conscience and Judaism, see Steven Schwarzchild, "Conscience," in *Contemporary Jewish Religious Thought* (New York: Charles Scribner's Sons, 1987), 87–90.

4. See Hannah Arendt, *On Violence* (San Diego: Harcourt Brace Jovanovich, 1969).

5. See Erich Fromm, *Escape from Freedom* (New York: Avon Books, 1941).

6. The classic example of internal authority is the Akeidah. God does not "force" Abraham; God "tests" him. Abraham voluntarily agrees to the sacrifice, thereby passing the test. Isaac is not forced to go to Moriah; he walks voluntarily. Similarly, Moses agrees to return to Egypt for the sake of liberating the Israelite slaves. God's role is purely that of an advocate. The model of prophetic exhortation is, according to Professor Yochanan Muffs, evidence that the biblical God persuades rather than coerces.

7. Michael Wyschogrod, *The Body of Faith: Judaism and Corporeal Election* (Minneapolis: Seabury Press, 1982), 191–97.

8. Not only love and fear but also fundamental drives—hunger, lust, or the desire for safety—present a sense of compulsion. Nonetheless, all people retain a choice of when to act on an urge, when to sublimate it, and when to deny it.

9. See "Ahavah" and "Yirat Shamayim" in *Otzar ha-Aggadah*, ed. Moshe David Gross (Jerusalem: Mossad ha-Rav Kook), 1:29–32 and 1:486–89.

10. Particularly among the Hasidei Ashkenaz, the pietistic Jews of medieval Franco-Germany. See Joseph Dan, *Jewish Mysticism and Jewish Ethics* (Seattle: University of Washington Press, 1986), ch. 3, and Yehudah heHasid, *Sefer Hasidim* (Jerusalem: Mossad ha-Rav Kook, 1983), 158–59.

11. See Abraham Millgram, *Jewish Worship* (Philadelphia: Jewish Publication Society, 1971), 461–63.

12. Joseph Soloveitchik, "The Lonely Man of Faith," *Tradition* 7, no. 2 (1965): 5–67.

13. This is true across the denominations. See the work of Irving Greenberg, Aviva Zornberg, and David Hartman among the Orthodox; Abraham Joshua Heschel, Neil Gillman, and Elliot Dorff among the Conservatives; Eugene Borowitz, Rachel Adler, and Lawrence Kushner among the Reform; Arthur Green among the post-denominationalists; and Zalman Schachter-Shalomi within Jewish renewal.

14. Maimonides, *Mishneh Torah*, Hilchot T'shuvah 10:5.

15. Gerson D. Cohen, "The Song of Songs and the Jewish Religious Mentality," in *The Samuel Friedland Lectures, 1960–1966* (New York: Jewish Theological Seminary, 1966).

16. See especially Hosea and Jeremiah.

17. Deuteronomy 26:17.

18. Leviticus 26:12. For the unconditional and permanent nature of God's commitment to Israel, see Leviticus 26:44–45: "Yet even then, when they are in the land of their enemies, I will not reject them or spurn them so as to destroy them, annulling my Covenant with them: for I, the Holy One, am their God. I will remember in their favor the Covenant with the ancients, whom I freed from the Land of Egypt in the sight of the nations to be their God: I, the Holy One."

19. Seder Eliyahu 70.

20. Mishnah Machshirin 1:3. See Jacob Neusner, *Form-Criticism and Exegesis* (Minneapolis: University of Minnesota Press, 1980).

21. The application and expansion of this idea are the basis of Bradley Shavit Artson, *It's a Mitzvah! Step-by-Step to Jewish Living* (West Orange, N.J., and New York: Behrman House and Rabbinical Assembly, 1995).

22. See, for example, Erik Erikson, *Childhood and Society* (New York: W. W. Norton, 1963).

23. Modern anthropology and sociology expand the claim, asserting that how we view God and how we structure religion emerge from a projection of our social structure. See Clifford Geertz, *The Interpretation of Cultures* (New York: Basic Books, 1973), 87–141, and William A. Leesa and Evon Z. Vogt, eds., *Reader in Comparative Religion: An Anthropological Approach* (New York: Harper and Row, 1979).

24. Cohen, 9.

25. Harold Schulweis, "Jewish Apartheid," *Moment*, December 1985, 23–28, and "Our House Divided: An Exchange," *Moment*, January–February 1986, 54–61.

26. Just what are the minimal standards is itself an important question. Why is it, for example, that Jews for Jesus are outside the boundaries of Jewish peoplehood whereas the Society for Humanistic Judaism is inside? Are our minimal standards exclusively negative (that is, rejecting other religions or the divinity of Jesus)?

27. At this point, it is important to state that this model for relationship as the central metaphor of Jewish theology has clear implications not merely for the legitimacy of various forms of Judaism but also for the empirical reality that different religions and cultures relate to the universe differently. Expecting them to meet the standards of Judaism is asking that friends meet the standards set for lovers. God relates differently to different cultures, and they fulfill the needs of their unique relationships on their own terms. The standards set for Christianity, for Islam, for Buddhism, are different, not illegitimate. See David Novak, *The Image of the Non-Jew in Judaism* (Lewiston, N.Y.: Edwin Mellen Press, 1983).

Glossary

aggadah, *pl.* **aggadot** Rabbinic legend or tale. Aggadot might be told as interpretations of biblical passages (Midrash Aggadah) or simply as a story of a sage or a contemporary.

Aḥaron aḥaron ḥaviv "The last is most precious."

ahavat haShem "Love of God."

avak l'shon hara "The dust of evil speech," a term describing comments that aren't explicitly derogatory but still elicit a negative response.

bikur ḥolim "Visiting the sick," one of Judaism's most compelling commandments.

B'reishit Rabbah Early rabbinic midrash on the book of Genesis.

ḥochmah "Wisdom."

ḥesed "Love," comparable to the English word grace. It is due to God's ḥesed that the people Israel received the Torah, and it is a reflection of our being made in the divine image that allows that is best exemplified by our showing ḥesed to each other.

ḥevruta "Fellowship; companionship."

ḥovah "Obligation."

k'dushah "Holiness." A term used to evoke the ideal of Jewish religious life, a sense of living in God's presence.

kiddushin "Holiness," a term used for a Jewish wedding ceremony.

klal Yisrael "All [the people] Israel," a term meant to include every Jew.

kohen, *pl.* **kohanim** A biblical priest or a descendant of a biblical priest of the family of Aaron.

Kohen Gadol "High Priest," the priest who performed the sacrificial services in the Temple in Jerusalem.

Kohelet The Hebrew name for the biblical book of Ecclesiastes.

kosher "Proper," a word that refers to the dietary laws established by the Torah as a mitzvah for all Jews. The practice of eating and preparing kosher food is kashrut.

l'shon hara "Evil speech," such as gossip, slander, or stereotyping.

massechet A volume of the Talmud.

menschlichkeit Yiddish word describing the character or quality of an ethical, decent, caring person—a mensch. Menschlichkeit is the characteristic of a mensch.

midot, *sing.,* **midah** "Values; virtues."

midrash, *pl.* **midrashim** "Searching," a word used to denote rabbinic exegesis of scripture; it can be both a genre (a midrash) and a collection of literature (the Midrash). The golden age of midrash lasted from late antiquity to the early medieval period.

Moshe Rabbenu "Moses Our Rebbe," a traditional way of referring to Moses.

motzi shem ra "Spreading a bad name," the act of repeating defaming information or opinions.

mum "Blemish; defect." A mum disqualifies both a *kohen* and an animal from participating in a valid sacrifice.

n'shamah "Soul." In the biblical period, the term indicated every aspect of one's total self, integrated and whole.

parashah A weekly reading from the Torah. The world over, every congregation of Jews reads the same selection as every other congregation, completing the reading of the entire Torah each calendar year and then beginning it again.

parochet "Curtain," specifically, the curtain concealing the Torah in the Holy Ark.

poskim, *fem.* **poskot** Rabbinic authorities on Jewish law.

p'shat Contextual meaning of a biblical verse.

rav "Rabbi," one's primary authority on religious observance and Jewish law.

r'chilut "Gossip." A statement can be r'chilut whether it is true or false, provided it is harmful to the subject of the statement.

rebbe, *pl.* **rebbe'im** A master teacher; a spiritual guide or mentor; one's primary authority on spiritual growth and character formation.

reshimu In kabbalah, the empty space into which God poured the divine energy to create all.

rofei han'fashot "Healers of souls," the phrase used by Maimonides to describe the role of sages and rabbis in the Jewish community.

Shabbat, *pl.* **Shabbatot** "The Sabbath," the day of rest, from sundown on Friday to sundown on Saturday, commemorating God's Creation of the world and God's liberation of the people Israel from Egyptian bondage. The mitzvah of observing Shabbat is recorded (among other places) in the Torah, at Exodus 20:8–11.

Sh'chinah "Presence," a term describing God in relationship with the world, humanity, or the people Israel. In later Jewish literature, Sh'chinah is perceived as a female manifestation of the Divine.

sh'leimut "Wholeness; completion."

sh'mirat halashon "Guarding the tongue," the mitzvah of refraining from slanderous, malicious, or harmful speech.

siddur "Prayer book."

Taḥanun "Petition," prayers added after the Amidah, the core prayers of the statutory worship service.

talmid, *pl.* **talmidim** "Disciple." The term can refer to one's student.

Talmud "Learning." The Talmud is an encyclopedic compilation of ancient rabbinic lore, law, philosophy, and theology. It is the fundamental document for all subsequent rabbinic Judaism and a model of a religiosity that respects argument, diverse viewpoints, and the role of reason in understanding as much of the truth as is possible.

tochaḥah "Rebuke." The mitzvah of rebuke is recorded in the Torah at Leviticus 19:17.

Torah "Teaching; instruction." In its most limited meaning, Torah refers to the Five Books of Moses (Genesis, Exodus, Leviticus, Numbers, Deuteronomy). In its broadest sense, Torah is the entirety of Jewish tradition and teaching.

tza'ar ba'alei ḥayim "The pain of living things." Judaism's commandment to care for all creatures in a way that minimizes their suffering and pain.

tzedek "Righteous." A tzaddik (*pl.* tzaddikim) is a righteous person who embodies the highest levels of ethical and ritual mitzvot.

tzimtzum "Contraction; withdrawal," a kabbalistic concept that God withdrew into a point of infinite density (or created an empty sphere) through which the world was created.

yetzer hara "The inclination for evil." Everyone has one. Channeling and harnessing it is our lifework.

yetzer hatov "The inclination for good." Everyone has one; cultivating it is our lifework.

yirat shamayim "Fear of heaven."

Index

Boldface indicates first appearance in the text of a glossed term.

About the Author

Rabbi Bradley Shavit Artson is the Dean of the Ziegler School of Rabbinic Studies and Vice President of the University of Judaism in Los Angeles, where he teaches ancient and medieval Jewish philosophy and senior homiletics. Rabbi Artson served as a congregational rabbi for ten years. He is the author of five books, well over one hundred articles, and a weekly e-mail commentary on the Torah portion that reaches some twelve thousand subscribers. Rabbi Artson is on the faculty of the Wexner Heritage Foundation, speaks frequently to UJA/Federation communities, and is a frequent lecturer and guest teacher. He earned his rabbinic ordination from the Jewish Theological Seminary, and his B.A. from Harvard University. Rabbi Artson lives in California with his wife, Elana, and their twins, Shira and Jacob. For more about Rabbi Artson, visit www.bradartson.com.